Taxing the Poor

THE AARON WILDAVSKY FORUM FOR PUBLIC POLICY

Edited by Lee Friedman

This series is to sustain the intellectual excitement that
Aaron Wildavsky created for scholars of public policy everywhere.
The ideas in each volume are initially presented and discussed
at a public lecture and forum held at the University of California.

AARON WILDAVSKY, 1930–1993

"Your prolific pen has brought real politics to the study of budgeting, to the analysis of myriad public policies, and to the discovery of the values underlying the political cultures by which peoples live. You have improved every institution with which you have been associated, notably Berkeley's Graduate School of Public Policy, which as Founding Dean you quickened with your restless innovative energy. Advocate of freedom, mentor to policy analysts everywhere." (Yale University, May 1993, from text granting the honorary degree of Doctor of Social Science)

Taxing the Poor

*Doing Damage to
the Truly Disadvantaged*

Katherine S. Newman and
Rourke L. O'Brien

UNIVERSITY OF CALIFORNIA PRESS

Berkeley   Los Angeles   London

University of California Press, one of the most distinguished university presses in the United States, enriches lives around the world by advancing scholarship in the humanities, social sciences, and natural sciences. Its activities are supported by the UC Press Foundation and by philanthropic contributions from individuals and institutions. For more information, visit www.ucpress.edu.

University of California Press
Berkeley and Los Angeles, California

University of California Press, Ltd.
London, England

Library of Congress Cataloging-in-Publication Data

Newman, Katherine S., 1953–
    Taxing the poor : doing damage to the truly disadvantaged / Katherine S. Newman and Rourke L. O'Brien.
        p.   cm.
    Includes bibliographical references and index.
    ISBN 978-0-520-26966-8 (cloth : alk. paper)—ISBN 978-0-520-26967-5 (pbk. : alk. paper)
    1. Poor—Taxation—Southern States. 2. Poor—Taxation—United States.
3. Poverty—Southern States. 4. Poverty—United States. I. O'Brien, Rourke L., 1984– II. Title.
HJ2387.N49   2011
336.20086'9420973—dc22   2010030723

Manufactured in the United States of America

20 19 18 17 16 15 14 13 12 11
10 9 8 7 6 5 4 3 2 1

This book is printed on Cascades Enviro 100, a 100% post-consumer waste, recycled, de-inked fiber. FSC recycled certified and processed chlorine free. It is acid free, Ecologo certified, and manufactured by BioGas energy.

*To the staff of Alabama Arise, who devote their lives
to the cause of tax justice for the poor*

To Paul and Kathleen O'Brien, for their love and support

CONTENTS

Conclusion: Are We Our Brothers' Keepers?
149

ILLUSTRATIONS

PHOTOGRAPHS
(all photos by the authors)

FIGURES

MAPS

TABLES

PREFACE

The origin of this book lies in a failed political campaign. In the fall of 2007, Alabama Arise, a coalition of congregations and organizations based in Montgomery, Alabama, mounted a campaign to persuade the state legislature to repeal the sales tax on food for home consumption, a levy that—between state and local taxation—was adding as much as 12 percent to consumers' grocery bills.[1] State taxes of this kind hit everyone—rich and poor—in the pocketbook. But Alabama citizens at the bottom of the economic ladder, living at the very edge of survival to begin with, were finding themselves unable to feed their families at the end of the month. Looking to stretch the dollar or the allotment of food stamps, poor families were going without or switching to cheap food that fills the stomach but leads to obesity and all the damaging consequences that follow.

Advocates of the tax repeal took to the airwaves of Alabama public television, buttonholed the editors of the leading newspapers, and rallied church folk committed to the cause. The tireless organizers of Alabama Arise fanned out all over the state—from rural trailer parks to the downtown business districts—corralling anyone who would listen, urging them to contact their legislators, handing out miniature grocery bags with election slogans printed on the side urging the repeal.

Twenty senators had promised their support. One more was needed to pull the measure over the threshold. While most senators wanted to lower the grocery tax, powerful lobbyists opposed the plan to pay for it—capping deductions for high-income taxpayers. Alabama Arise and their legislative sponsor, Representative John F. Knight, Jr. (D-Montgomery), were cautiously optimistic, since they had been down this road before. In 2003, the legislature had passed a sweeping tax reform package. Yet the provisions of the Alabama constitution require that even a local tax ordinance that clears the legislature must be put to a statewide public referendum. That year, the powers opposed to the initiative saturated the airwaves with dire warnings of tax increases if it passed: "We're taxed enough. Just say no!" Ironically, most poor Alabamians are overtaxed by the state's regressive system, and the reform package would have reduced their burden while increasing the hit to high-income people and big corporations. Naysayers were so successful that many of Alabama's hard-pressed poor—who own no property and would have benefited from lower income taxes—voted against the bill, and it went down to defeat.

This time, however, Arise was convinced they had a winning strategy. Instead of going after comprehensive reform of income, sales, and property taxes, they proposed a modest plan: eliminating the state portion of the grocery tax, expanding family-friendly income tax deductions, and capping a lopsided deduction that benefited those at high incomes. Lamenting how bad grocers feel when customers can't pay the cashier and have to put food back on the shelf, the Alabama Grocers Association threw its support behind the bill. The requisite three-fifths vote seemed within reach; only one more senator was needed. To the lasting disappointment of the reformers, none of the opponents broke ranks. The measure failed once again, leaving Alabama, one of the poorest states in the country, with the dubious distinction of being one of only two states to exact the full sales tax on food. For the poor and the near poor, the consequences are dire.

. . .

Beatrice Coleman is one of the millions of Alabama residents for whom a break on the cost of food would make an enormous difference. Mother of two teens, Bea struggles with a mountain of health problems—asthma, obstructive pulmonary lung disease, diabetes, and a degenerative bone disease crippling her back— and none of this is made better by a poor diet, devoid of fresh fruit and vegetables and loaded with carbohydrates, which is all that Bea can afford to buy with the disability checks she receives every month. Her weight grows worse by the week, stressing her spine and making it painful to walk or bend. Disability is her only source of income, since her condition makes it impossible to work at the kinds of jobs for which she is qualified.

Bea hails from rural New Mexico, one of five children in a family that was stable and secure in her early years. "We grew up on a farm," she explains. "My mom did the farming and was the homemaker; my dad worked in the Kerr-McGee [uranium] mines [which were] close to my hometown. It was pretty fun. I remember waking up in the morning and going to get the eggs from the chickens, riding the horses, and feeding the cows." Bea's parents owned the farm, since her father made good money

Beatrice Coleman worked as a nursing assistant but hurt her back and is now disabled, with two teenagers to support on her own.

in the mines. Thinking back, she describes a world of fresh air, plenty of food, vigorous days full of chores, boisterous siblings, and a mother who was happy and loving. The memories bring a smile to her face, but it doesn't last. Paradise came to an abrupt end, and, in a sense, the long march toward the difficult life she leads now started when her childhood imploded. "I lived [on the farm] until I was about seven and they got divorced," Bea explained. "We moved into the city of Grants, New Mexico. It was just my mom and the five of us children in a trailer. It was really, really hard. She was on welfare and food stamps. . . . We had to . . . find copper [to sell] just to get our next meal a lot of nights. It was just bread and bologna."

With tears spilling down her cheeks, Bea remembers how her mother went to bed hungry so that she could give what food she had to her children. Bea's mother moved the family again to be closer to her parents, but they proved to be of little assistance. It was Bea's first lesson in what it means to be alone with mounting troubles. "I remember when I was about eight years old, my sister asked my dad for a dollar to buy some bread. He told her 'you and your mom can go eat crap.'"

Bea worships her mother, who managed "every day to make it up," to entertain her children by cloaking their poverty in games and little contests. Who can find the most cans to redeem? What treat can we make out of beans today? In recognition of this heroic struggle, Bea now calls her mother every day, relies on her advice, and honors her by confiding her own sorrows in the one person who remains a rock. Back in the day, though, Bea wasn't quite this attentive or respectful. Mostly, she was looking for an escape: from school, from discipline, and from the shame and hardship of life in that trailer park. At seventeen she ran away with a boy from her school, got pregnant, and found herself a single mother with no money and no skills. She left her boyfriend before her daughter was born because he beat her. Four months after the first baby arrived, she found herself pregnant by another man who, it turned out, was no better than the first.

For many women, a history like this would be a one-way ticket to a life on welfare. Bea refused that fate. Indeed, the determination so visible in her today began to emerge—as is often the case for poor single mothers—when the full weight of responsibility for two children became clear. She insisted she would find a way to be self-sufficient, and in short order, this ninth-grade dropout passed her GED exam and went to work for a firm that provides home care for people with disabilities. "I would work ten days straight, have one day off, and then go back for another ten days. I would work the graveyard shift, go home and shower, take the kids to school or day care, and then go back to work. I did that for four years."

Working around the clock for so little money seemed an endless burden. Bea knew that she would never see a more lucrative paycheck if she didn't go back to school to qualify for a better job. She made up her mind to go back to college to become a certified nursing assistant (CNA), the first step in a long road toward becoming a registered flight nurse, a first responder who rides helicopters to the scenes of major accidents. CNAs are the infantry of the nursing profession. Hard physical labor—dressing patients who cannot move, bending all day to strip bed linens, helping disabled people to their feet—is a routine part of their daily grind. Women in good physical shape find the job tough on their bodies. Bea was not one of them. She has had a weight problem most of her life. It was not improved by a diet of canned vegetables, bologna loaded with salt, and filling but calorie-laden mac and cheese, with a Kool-Aid chaser. Much as she tried to modify her intake, the pounds piled on, and the physical stress of the job began to take its toll.

"One day I tried to lift a lady by myself," she recalled. "I was moving her towards me so I could change the sheets underneath her, and I heard a 'pop.'" A searing pain ran through her lower back, and Bea knew right then and there that she was in trouble. The next day she found her way to a clinic, where the harried doctor on call told her, "It's your weight. Just lose that weight and you'll be fine."

The pain was intense and unrelenting. The doctor's admonition made Bea think perhaps it was all "in her head," so she went back to work. Her condition just got worse. Eventually she was diagnosed with degenerative joint disease in her back, with arthritis and stenosis, which means that her spine is closing up. The orthopedist she saw, after months and months of painkillers, told Bea she would be in a wheelchair by the age of thirty.

Poverty tends to be overdetermined. Problems that drive people into life at the bottom come from all directions. Trying to cope with children alone, with no help from their fathers, adds

Bea's rental house is in a poor neighborhood surrounded by abandoned properties marked with "do not trespass" signs.

to the stress that physically demanding jobs visit on women who are having trouble making ends meet. Worrying about being evicted or making the car payments that enable them to get to work at all does not help. Above all, though, a debilitating health condition, one that instantly compromises a parent's job, creates a powerful downdraft right into homelessness or the need to throw oneself into the arms of anyone who will offer some help.

In Bea's case, the one to offer help was her first legal husband, who promised to care for her and her two children but ended up stealing from her to feed his crack cocaine habit. She threw him out and has been on her own ever since. She is not satisfied, not at all. Her neighborhood is dangerous, filled with abandoned houses and shady characters. Gunshots ring out in the alley behind her home. Bea's kids have been jumped twice in the last two years; her sister-in-law was murdered. Bea is certain that racial tension is a factor in all the violence, since people in her neighborhood, entirely black and poor, think she is white although she is actually Hispanic.

How will Bea ever get her life back on track? Education. But how is a disabled mother to get to school, much less pay the tuition bill? Millions of other poor Americans—especially those in the rural regions of states like Alabama—face the same question. Increasingly, the answer comes back in the form of online, for-profit degrees that people like Bea are hoping will pave the way to a job that pays. "Two years ago, I kept seeing advertisements on TV for Virginia College online," she explains, "and I thought, 'that might be something I can do' because I . . . know how to use a computer. So I went back to school. I typed in my information into the computer and by the time I could push *send*, Virginia College was on the phone with me. I [thought] wow, that's fast. They are really trying to help me! So I went back to school."

Bea's face lights up with confidence and purpose when she talks about the degree she is studying for in medical billing. She is certain it will lead to a good job, one that might pay as much as $15 an hour, far more than anything she has ever earned. Yet the price tag is daunting. Virginia College is charging her more than $4,000 a semester. By the time she completes the course work they require, Bea will be nearly $40,000 in debt, a staggering sum of money for someone with her monthly income.

The tuition costs are coming out of multiple loans from the federal government as part of its Stafford guaranteed loan program. In this, Bea is joining millions of other students who are up to their ears in debt to pay for an education whose payoff is hard to forecast. According to the College Board, 53 percent of students in the for-profit sector end up with cumulative debts of over $30,000. Even the nation's most costly private schools do not see statistics like this.[2] Many for-profit colleges provide

The online, for-profit college Bea enrolled in has charged her nearly $40,000 for a four-year course in medical billing. On a good day, she puts in ten hours of study at the computer.

valuable services to nontraditional students, and the very best of them may even outdo community college vocational programs in terms of job placement. But quality control is hard to exercise, particularly with consumers who are isolated and unable to access information about the track record of a college like Bea's.[3]

Should Bea be unable to land a high-paying job, she will find it hard to discharge her mounting pile of federal student loans. Credit card debt can be forgiven in a bankruptcy filing, but federal law protects loans secured to pay for education.[4] Of the seventy-two thousand federal student loan borrowers who entered bankruptcy in 2008, a mere 0.4 percent tried to get a special dispensation of this kind. Only 22 percent of them were able to convince a bankruptcy judge that they should be freed of the burden.[5] Bea will spend the rest of her life trying to clear this debt, and it will only be affordable—barely—if she is fortunate enough to land the job she is hoping for.

There is very little slack in her budget otherwise. Her household survives on roughly $1,500 a month, composed of disability payments, SSI survivor benefits for her kids,[6] and $150 in food stamps. With this total in hand, she must find a way to cover $500 in rent, utility bills that frequently run north of $600, and a modest clothing budget (augmented by hand-me-downs) for her growing children.

It would help, in a million ways, if her food costs did not eat so deeply into her pocketbook. Thanks to the foresight of the federal government, Bea does not have to pay tax on food she buys with food stamps. But that allotment only covers $150 of the $400 she spends every month on food. The other $250 is taxed. For every $100 she spends in the Piggly Wiggly store that is about half a mile from her home, Bea pays an extra $10 to the state of Alabama. This sounds modest to a middle-class reader, but Bea is down to pennies by the end of the month. She cannot afford fresh fruit, relies on canned vegetables, and indulges in sugared cereals because that's what her kids will eat (and she doesn't want to waste money on things they won't touch). Bea fills her supermarket cart with processed bologna and mixes the hamburger she can afford—the high-fat-content version—with Ramen noodles. Her children *never* see real fruit juice; they do see bright pink soda when there is money for a treat. White bread and pasta are staples in her household. Canned spaghetti sauce and processed cheese line her shelves. Bea is careful, almost surgical, in her effort to save and stretch, but the kind of economizing she can afford is leading straight to a diet that creates obesity. When she gets home from the store, she sits down at the computer and puts in a ten-hour work day trying to earn her diploma. The combination of this poor diet and her enforced sedentary life multiplies her health problems.

Piggly Wiggly is one of the larger chains of grocery stores in Alabama.

Bea shops carefully to make her money last. She rarely buys fresh food, since canned goods are less expensive.

	05/07/10	3:45:34 PM
HUNT'S KETCH	$1.19	TF
(STORE SAVINGS	$0.10)	
RAGU SPAG SAUCE	$1.67	TF
(STORE SAVINGS	$0.68)	
TAMPICO PEACH/OR	$2.69	TF
TAMPICO STRAWBER	$2.69	TF
FLORDIA ORANGES	$5.99	TF
BANANAS	$1.07	TF
2.18 lb @ $0.49/lb		

FS Total	$86.59	# of items	45

Subtotal	$86.59
Total Tax	$8.66
Balance Due	$95.25

Food for home consumption is taxed at 10 percent in Birmingham. Bea has to pay almost $9 more for this shopping trip.

Bea is emotionally fragile; she is on the verge of tears much of the time. Taking a deep breath in order to get through her story, she speaks wistfully about how she would give anything to be able to take her son and daughter away from this dangerous neighborhood, how much she would like them to have birthday presents and new clothes like the more fortunate kids they know. We peeked into her son's bedroom, and she proudly showed us a new skateboard that her church provided him last Christmas. "My daughter says she's tired of being poor," Bea confides, and it clearly breaks her heart and redoubles her determination to finish her college course so that she can do something about their circumstances.

The weekend of our visit with Bea coincided with Mother's Day, a major holiday for Alabama families. Older people travel many miles to be with their moms on that special day. Most teenagers are oblivious, but not Bea's son. "Without you, I wouldn't be here," he wrote in a text message that arrived while our tape recorder was spinning. "Thank you for everything you have done for me. I know I get you upset sometimes, but we work things out as a family. So I want to appreciate you for having me. Happy Mother's Day. I love you forever."

Many a comfortable middle-class mother would be happy to get such a note.

One might argue that poor families like Bea's have so many problems to contend with that a 10 percent state and local tax on food is nothing more than a drop in a bucket already full to the brim with trouble. True. Some would observe that women who have little education and who support children without steady partners are likely to be in trouble no matter what the tax policy. Debatable, but a perspective one hears often enough from conservative corners. Yet many of the people whose lives we chronicle in this book found themselves struggling after a lifetime of working. In Pine Apple, Alabama, we met men and women who had put in twenty years at lumber plants and textile mills. The spread of deindustrialization throughout the country has left a lot of distress in its wake. It is hard enough for people who live in generous Northern states to adjust to these hardships. We see better outcomes in almost all measures of poverty among the poor in the North than we do if we look at the poor below the Mason-Dixon Line or, increasingly, to the west of the Rockies.

Alabama and Mississippi exact the highest sales tax levies from the poor, but they are not alone. Most southern states rely on regressive taxation of this kind and have done so for decades. Property taxes are the mirror image: they are very low and have been that way for a very long time. Regressive taxation in the South allows wealthy people to escape heavy taxes while the poor are disproportionately burdened by them, to the detriment of their longevity, health, education, and family structure. Understanding the relationship between these two trends—taxes and poverty-related outcomes—is the mission of this book.

·　　·　　·

Poverty in the United States is often associated with the history of the northern Rust Belt. Decades of deindustrialization, the decline of unions that once ruled the factories of Detroit and Gary, the growth of African American ghettos in the big cities—all of these forces shaped the experience of the poor in the North. Arguably, poverty is far more severe—and has been for decades—in the small towns and rural regions of the American South. Nearly 40 percent of the nation's poor people—and nearly five million of its poor children—live in the states of the old Confederacy.[7]

They live in places like Vrendenburgh, Alabama, two hours southwest of Montgomery, where we visited in May of 2010 to speak with people who feel the brunt of consumption taxes. The Quarters is a black settlement in Vrendenburgh composed of trailers and wooden shacks sitting high atop stilts that protect them from flooding. Some of the roads that wind through the district are paved; others are dirt tracks. Most of the trailers are neatly maintained, but every so often, one catches a glimpse of one that is rusted over, boarded up, and consumed by thick shrubs. A sign announcing Mama Sally's dangles from one of the wooden houses on the main street, but it appears to have been closed for months. Couples, teenagers, and children sit outside the trailers on makeshift porches, watching the young men repair old cars at the side of the road. There are no suburban lawns here, no sidewalks, no fire hydrants, and no schools nearby. Kids congregate at the church or a child care center in a double-wide trailer maintained by the Catholic sisters of the Edmundite Southern Missions. Sister Pat Flass pointed toward a cement court outside with a picnic table or two and noted with pride that only last year they had found the money to build an open-air roof over the tables so that families could eat outside and not bake in the southern sun.

Wooden houses in the Quarters, the black enclave of Vrendenburgh, Alabama. The stilts protect the houses from flooding.

The worn sign announces "Mama Sally's" tavern on the small main street of the Quarters.

Sister Pat Flass, the outreach minister for the Edmundite Southern Missions, in the trailer that serves as a library and after-school center for children of the Quarters.

Vrendenburgh is forty miles from the nearest highway. Those who have cars can get to small towns fifteen or twenty miles down the road; those who don't, live in isolation. No one drives through Vrendenburgh without a reason, because it isn't on the way to anywhere. There is one store that sells food and gas within walking distance of the Quarters. James, the white man behind the till, has been responsible for this family business for many years. He knows all the customers, their kids, their parents, and their troubles. James keeps a large lined notebook full of the names of his customers and the running accounts they rack up. People rarely actually pay money for the goods they purchase; they just keep a tab, and when their checks come in—disability, Temporary Assistance for Needy Families (TANF), Social Security, and the

Most houses in the Quarters are trailers, but a few are wooden "shotgun shacks," named for their narrow width and floor plan through which one could shoot a straight shot. At some time in the past, houses were taxed according to their width, leading to a proliferation of shotgun shacks in black neighborhoods.

occasional paycheck—they settle their debts with James. Neither of us had ever seen this practice outside of movies of small-town life in the Great Depression, when no one had money and store-keepers did what they could to keep poor families afloat. But it is the way business is done in Vrendenburgh, and without James's willingness to wait, there wouldn't be any business at all.

One of the reasons James has to keep the "Big Book" is that he can no longer accept food stamps for any purchase in his store. Several years ago, inspectors arrived from a state agency whose name he could no longer remember and pulled the authority to receive food stamps right out from under James and his brother-in-law, who runs a similar store in another hamlet. The owners

The only store within walking distance of the Quarters no longer takes food stamps and has very little to offer customers. The shelves hold a sparse collection of dry goods, canned goods, cereals, and candy.

were accused of fraud, the ostensible reason for depriving them of food stamp business. James protests that he has all the proper receipts for food stamp accounts and opines that the inspectors were just looking for an excuse to force people to spend their food stamps in stores with lower prices and greater economies of scale. He doesn't quite say that the big stores were behind the inspection, but it's an unspoken possibility.

In any case, the consequences of this decision are serious for the citizens of Vrendenburgh. Food stamps are a lifeline; most residents of the Quarters simply don't have the money to eat without them, particularly since the factories that once employed them have collapsed under the weight of the recession that began in 2007. Unable to spend food stamps in James's store, they are forced to dig into their meager reserves to afford a shopping trip. Those who have cars spend precious dollars filling the gas tank to get to a Piggly Wiggly store in a distant town. Those who don't must rely on their neighbors, who are generally willing to drive those without wheels—for a price: $20 seems to be the going rate.

Rural isolation imposes particularly heavy burdens on the poor. Every service they need—electricity to run air-conditioning units in a place where the summer is unbearably hot and humid, drinking water, heating oil in the winter—is more expensive because they are so far from the centers of distribution. If it takes 5 percent of their food budget just to make one trip to the store, they realize they have to shop carefully, filling the cart not with fresh food that will spoil in time, but with canned or dried goods that will last for a month. No surprise that so many people walking around Vrendenburgh are heavy, from the children to the grandparents. The Catholic sisters tell us that the diseases afflicting the overweight are rampant here. Perhaps we should not be surprised. The community feels like a place the rest of us have forgotten and the world has left behind. As the special education teacher in the area, Vendell Palmer, told us, only one generation back these folks made a living picking crops for white farmers, ate what they could grow themselves, and had no running water. Vendell herself was one of seven children of a single mother, and she knows from personal experience about hardship.

It is tempting to assume that the central issue in this book—the impact of regressive taxation—is of relevance only to the very poor. Not so. On the eastern side of Montgomery, we drove to the small town near the Tuskegee Institute of Booker T. Washington fame.[8] Gail Wyman and her extended family have lived in this part of Alabama for many generations. The Wymans, devoted members of the local Baptist church whose service we attended with Gail when our interview was over, join a congregation of white families engaged with Christian charity and friendly with the African American congregations down the road. A small community of fewer than one thousand people, Gail's town is proud and well kept but hardly exploding with economic growth.

Gail graduated from high school in the late 1990s and married her sweetheart, and together they have been raising a family that now includes two children. When Gail finished junior college and got an associate of sciences degree, she parlayed her part-time job working for a local dentist into a full-time position as the medical office business manager. She has worked there for seven years now. After taxes and medical insurance, her take-home pay is about $1,800 a month. While her husband was steadily employed, the family was able to pay the mortgage on their trailer, take care of the child care bills for their youngest, a little boy of four, and have enough money to spare for an occasional night on the town.

For reasons Gail was too embarrassed to explain, her husband had quit his job in a dry-cleaning shop six months earlier. She swallowed hard and tried to hold back her tears as she explained that he had been unable to find a job of any kind to replace it. All of a sudden, the Wyman family found itself on the edge of a financial abyss. "Our biggest expense is our house payment of $350 a month," she explained, "and then we have a car payment of $389. I pay 50 percent of my family health insurance, $361 a month, $86 for dental, $29 for hospitalization insurance. Food is quite expensive for four people. I would say at least $80 a week, maybe a little more. Preschool is about $100 a month for each of my children."

By the end of the month, her $1,800 is totally exhausted. Her family is enrolled in the federal Women, Infants, and Children (WIC) program, which provides some basic foodstuffs for children: milk and eggs, cereal, bread, peanut butter or dried beans, juice, and a produce voucher worth $6 a month. WIC is only for children under the age of five, which means they will lose this supplement in less than a year. They have been on WIC since she was pregnant with her first child; it helped to provide baby formula when he was an infant and she was at work. This program was critical to the Wymans even when Gail's husband was employed. Now that he is out of work, it is a lifeline she cannot quite imagine having to forgo. She has never applied for food stamps and doesn't think she would qualify with her income. "It is very overwhelming at times, and stressful," Gail said quietly. "To not know where it's coming from.... We're very thrifty with our money. We don't spend it on a lot of extras, only the necessities." They don't buy clothes or toys for the kids like they used to, and she doesn't spend a dime on herself. She takes on extra jobs on the weekends and nights, working for a woman who has a babysitting business. That can bring in as much as $50 on a good weekend, but she hasn't had any calls this month. Their savings are all gone, and they avoid debt by not having a credit card. They are independent and too proud to ask their parents for help, but they may get to the point where they have no choice.

·   ·   ·

The rural South is another country for those of us familiar with ghetto poverty in the big cities of the Northeast. We think we know what poverty looks like, but we rarely see anything like the conditions in Pine Apple or Vrendenburgh, Alabama. Even in Tuskegee, which is huge by comparison to the smaller settlements we visited, the cost of filling a gas tank, purchasing a basket of groceries, or buying a T-shirt can be as much as 30 percent more than in Montgomery or Birmingham. Rural isolation is not the only reason why people are so hard up, though. They are also paying over the mark because the food bill, the clothing tab, medications, and virtually everything else are all subject to sales taxes that are higher than anywhere else in the country.

The life of a poor child is therefore powerfully affected by decisions made at the state and local levels. The money left in parents' pockets after all of these policies are taken into account is a direct consequence of the way in which the child's state of residence resolves these fiscal (and very political) questions. A poor child in Harlem and the child's counterpart in Selma face very different resource baskets, even when their parents earn the same salaries. Differences in the cost of living close this gap to a degree, but even after taking into account how expensive housing, clothing, and other essentials are in New York, compared to Alabama, a gulf remains. Virtually everything that matters in determining the life chances of America's children—what kind of diet their parents can put on the table, how often they can be taken to the doctor, whether their classrooms have state-of-the-art laboratories or textbooks that were out of date in the 1960s— is affected by how their families are taxed.

Tax policy is rarely discussed by scholars interested in the depth and demography of poverty. Some sociologists have drawn inspiration from the work of Joseph Schumpeter, catalyzing a new fiscal sociology[9] that focuses attention on the comparative history of tax policy as an aspect of state development,[10] but this nascent movement does not dwell on the problem of poverty. To the extent that students of poverty have considered taxation, we hear more about the Earned Income Tax Credit (EITC) than any other element of tax policy. The EITC has been a successful means of delivering more take-home pay to low-wage workers, but it is hardly the only aspect of the tax code that deserves attention.

Bread-and-butter questions that preoccupy politicians—income and property taxes, sales and excise taxes, particularly at the state and local levels—are largely the province of applied policy analysts at the Urban Institute or the Center on Budget and Policy Priorities. With the notable (and admirable) exception of Isaac Martin, whose recent work on the history of property tax revolts is essential reading for students of tax policy and politics,[11] sociologists have not engaged this issue.

Economists interested in public finance and law professors who dwell on the intricacies of taxation are generally preoccupied with federal statutes. Yet it is at the state and local levels that a good deal of the important action takes place. School funding, Medicaid eligibility, and forms of social assistance—from welfare stipends to unemployment insurance and child health insurance coverage—are all under the control of legislatures far from Washington. States decide what kinds of expenses are deductible against their tax bills, and deductibles vary dramatically between generous states—which provide renter's credits, refundable earned income and child tax credits, subsidies for utilities bills, and the like—and states that offer meager support for the poor and provide none of the above.

The tax story is important to absorb, even for poverty scholars interested in the more traditional problems of earnings or wealth distribution. The kind of labor market that developed in Boston or Memphis has a great deal to do with the history of state and local investments—and the tax base required to make them. Hostility to labor unions, low levels of unemployment benefits, generous tax breaks to firms—all of these local decisions influence what kinds of businesses locate in the Southwest or the Northeast. As Barry Bluestone and Bennett Harrison showed decades ago,[12] long before the offshoring of high-wage jobs to low-wage countries began, the country witnessed an internal migration of manufacturing out of the unionized states of Michigan or Ohio, to the nonunion states of Georgia or South Carolina, particularly in textile and auto manufacturing. Firms were seeking more than an escape from union contracts; they were on the lookout for states with low business taxes.

While the analysis of industrial settlement patterns is beyond our purview and has been studied extensively by historians, we mention this point to indicate that the fiscal structure of the states is hardly the only force at work in shaping the lives of the poor. The presence or absence of high-paying industries determines opportunities available in the labor market. States that invest heavily in education—from elementary schools to public universities—are able to develop a workforce that commands much higher wages. These structural factors condition the earnings that mothers and fathers can bring to the table. In shining a light on tax policy, we do not mean to minimize the more traditional concerns social scientists have about educational attainment, income, or wealth.

Moreover, because the southern states are poor in comparison to the rest of the country, it is quite likely that they end up taxing the poor heavily in part because they have to derive revenue from all comers. Sadly, though, the deeper the southern states (and increasingly those in the West) dig into the pocketbooks of low-income families, the more they exacerbate the very problems we associate with poverty in the first place: low levels of educational attainment, single-parent households, crime, and the like. An endless vortex of taxation, social problems, poverty, and more taxation seems to follow.

Scholars of poverty know a great deal about the social patholo-
gies we focus on here as outcomes but have not looked at the role
of taxation in this picture. Our purpose, then, is to direct attention to regional variation in poverty patterns and to argue that a
powerful source of divergence between the southern states and
much of the rest of the United States is to be found in the ways in
which they tax the poor. We will show that these regional differences are long-standing and are reinforced by supermajority voting rules and constitutional limits on public sector spending that,
in many cases, date back to the Jim Crow era. The spread of these
laws throughout the southern states meant that the region entered
the period of rising inequality (from the mid-1970s onward) with
a more egregious poverty problem than any other part of the
country.

That legacy has cost the southern states dearly and—as we
show in chapter five—is placing a heavy burden on the rest of
the country as well. We will attempt to measure that burden in
terms of excess mortality, higher rates of teen pregnancy, lower
educational attainment, and higher crime. These characteristics
are well-known features of the poverty landscape. We will show
that they are worse—significantly worse—in the states of the old
Confederacy and that tax policies that rob the poor of disposable
income are causally related to these debilitating outcomes.

To understand how this pattern came into existence, we begin
with a look at the history of taxation in the South and contrast
it with the rest of the country. The pattern is distinctive and
destructive. It is also not simply a matter of policy history. The
problem is very much with us today, in part because—as we show
in chapter 2—very high barriers to change are in place throughout the South and have been for decades. Proposition 13—the
1978 tax revolt that lowered property taxes in California and put

in place extraordinary obstacles to raising them again—strangled the public sector. Yet the South began erecting similar hurdles as far back as the nineteenth century. In chapter 3, we examine just how poor the South is and what kinds of consequences income poverty has for the regional concentration of pernicious health outcomes, low levels of educational attainment, and other variables that are often associated with (and that help to perpetuate) poverty. We then ask, in chapter 4, what role regressive taxation has played in intensifying these outcomes and show that it has been a powerful driver.

If this were merely a story about how the pre–civil rights era divided southern social policy from that of the rest of the country, we might be able to chalk up the problem to a long period of recovery needed for the region to catch up. Unfortunately, as we show in chapter 5, as recently as the last twenty-five years, the southern states have bucked a tide prompted by the federal government to lower the tax burden on the poor. And the South is no longer alone in its reliance on regressive taxation. After Proposition 13 changed the tax system in California, supermajority rules and constitutional limitations on spending spread throughout the western states, leading to a pronounced reliance on sales tax—which hammers the poor—in yet another region. What is this costing the country in lost lives, education forgone, and children born to fragile families? We take time to show what a difference it would make if that had not happened, by simulating the poverty-related outcomes as they would appear if the South taxed its poor citizens at the median level or, even more dramatically, at the level the northeastern states use. In the end, we conclude that the only real hope for breaking this cycle, which so powerfully constrains the fates of millions of poor families, is to move the safety net out of the hands of the states.

ACKNOWLEDGMENTS

This book examines a little-known history of regional differences in the way we tax the poor and the consequences of these policies for the nation's least fortunate citizens. To investigate the twists and turns of arcane national, state, and local practices of this kind over the course of about 150 years, we had to stretch in many different directions. Since this is not a topic that has been explored before, we had to gather data on how much poor families pay in taxes on the goods they need to survive and figure out how the political history of the southern (and later the western) states laid the groundwork for supermajority rules and constitutional limits on spending. This required us to master data and forms of historical scholarship that were unfamiliar to us and to most other academics. Without the kindness of an army of fellow scholars, think tank compatriots, and policy specialists, it would never have been possible.

We are indebted first and foremost to the leadership of Alabama Arise, particularly Kimble Forrister and Brenda Boman and their organizers in Birmingham and Montgomery, especially Shakita Jones and Sister Pat Flass, the Outreach Minister for the Edmundite Southern Missions in Pine Apple, Alabama. These good people led us to the men and women whose voices appear in what would otherwise be a book of statistics. Cordelia Alexander, Alicia Smith, Beatrice Coleman, Rodney King, Tony and Senora Boddie, sisters Marlo and Lailo Finklea and their neighbors in "the Quarters," Floretta James, Nedopha and John Hobbs, and Pine Apple's special education teacher, Vendell Palmer, as well as several other citizens who prefer to be anonymous, shared the difficulties of life at the razor's edge of poverty with us. These interviews brought up painful realities that hardship produces among people who are struggling to provide for their families on a meager income in isolated rural settings, where getting to the grocery store can cost a woman with almost nothing to her name $20 in gas.

Together with Alabama State Representative John F. Knight (D-Montgomery), a champion of tax reform on behalf of the poor, our friends at Alabama Arise enabled us to meet with these families, educated us on the campaign, and hosted us with congeniality. We are pleased to dedicate royalties from the sale of *Taxing the Poor* to this worthy organization in the hope that these funds will help provide some of the resources needed to keep up the struggle.

This book was written at the invitation of our colleagues at the Goldman School of Public Policy at the University of California, Berkeley, who invited us to deliver the 2010 Wildavsky Lecture on which *Taxing the Poor* is based. Dean Henry Brady, Professors Lee Friedman, Ruckers Johnson, Jane Mauldon, and long-time friend Robert Reich welcomed us to Berkeley—as did sociologists Cybelle Fox, Margaret Weir, and Sandra Smith—and provided helpful criticisms of the manuscript. We are grateful for the invitation and the opportunity to benefit from such a thorough review. Our editor at UC Press, Naomi Schneider, added to the occasion by requesting two of the most helpful commentaries we received, from the distinguished Berkeley historian Robin Einhorn and the equally remarkable Stanford sociologist David Grusky. Though they were anonymous at the time, they subsequently responded to our request to thank them by name.

Two think tanks in Washington, DC, were critical resources in that they helped us assemble the data needed to understand exactly what the poor pay in taxes. Kevin Hassett and Alex Wein of the American Enterprise Institute had already been studying changing patterns of federal and state taxation of low-income families, and without the foundation they provided, the additional empirical work we did would not have been possible. The same must be said of Bob McIntyre and his colleagues at Citizens for Tax Justice.

We were lucky to be able to conduct several dry runs for the Wildavsky lecture in the company of colleagues at Princeton in the Center for the Study of Democratic Politics (run by Larry Bartels) and the sociology department's weekly seminar in economic sociology. There are far too many friends and colleagues at Princeton to thank each one by name, but we would like to single out Professor Scott Lynch, without whom we would not have known how to think about some difficult technical issues in the study of social impacts. We pulled scholars of the family from Princeton, Columbia, and Johns Hopkins together one afternoon to review our early findings on the impact of taxation on out-of-wedlock births, and hence we owe thanks to Sara McLanahan and Irv Garfinkle, Andrew Cherlin, and Jeanne Brooks-Gunn. Nancy Adler, the director of the MacArthur Foundation Network on Socio-Economic Status and Health, gave Katherine a chance to present some results on the health front at the final gathering of that group in Sonoma. Thanks go especially to Ichiro Kawachi, Michael Marmot, Mark Cullen, Karen Matthews, Ana Diez Roux, Bruce McEwen, Bill Dow, David Williams, and Teresa Seeman.

We had the opportunity to debut this project at the Stanford Center for the Study of Poverty and Inequality, where we had the good fortune to make the acquaintance of economic historian Gavin Wright, who knows more about the development of the South than anyone else in the profession, and we were fortunate to benefit from his review of the manuscript. Sociologists Paula England, Prudence Carter, Monica McDermott, Shelley Correll, Mark Granovetter, Tomas Jimenez, Cecilia Ridgeway, and Sean Reardon joined their fearless center leader, David Grusky, to give us a chance to run these ideas past a very stimulating crowd.

The unorthodox nature of this project required the indispensable input of a large network of colleagues who were kind enough to drop everything to provide us with reactions to our analyses as they were emerging. First among these scholars is Professor Christopher Jencks at Harvard's Kennedy School of Government. It would be almost impossible to ferret out the number of ideas in this book that owe their origins to his insights, as is true of so much that is valuable in contemporary sociology. The same might be said of Sheldon Danziger at the University of Michigan, who never says no to a request for a thoughtful reaction to an outlandish idea and runs the very best shop in the country for studying the impact of inequality. To his colleagues David Harding, Jim Hines, Dan Silverman, Mary Corcoran, and Brian Jacob we offer our gratitude and willingness to return the compliment. Tim Smeeding at the University of Wisconsin, Madison, has been unfailing in offering his advice, help, and above all an invaluable set of research contacts who have helped us along the way, especially Jonathan Fisher, who assisted us with the data from the Consumer Expenditure Survey.

In Cambridge, we were fortunate to run our ideas past Bruce Western, Kathryn Edin, and Peter Diamond. Our Columbia colleagues Eric Foner and Ira Katznelson reviewed the historical chapter and gave us many insights into the racial and populist politics of the antebellum and New Deal South. We would have made many more mistakes if it had not been for the corrections of historian Steven Attewell at the University of California, Santa Barbara. For that matter, the book simply would not exist without the constant methodological and substantive contributions of his father, Paul Attewell, Professor of Sociology at the City University of New York Graduate Center. We learned just about everything we know about the intricacies of fixed-effects models from Paul and would have been completely at sea had he not overseen the analyses that appear in chapters 4 and 5.

We thank Princeton graduate students Elizabeth Derickson, who produced all of the maps in the volume, and David Pedulla, who contributed important methodological insights. Joanne Golann scoured newspaper archives for articles that helped us understand public reactions to tax increases in the southern states throughout the twentieth century. *Taxing the Poor* was written during Katherine Newman's tenure as the Malcolm Forbes Class of 1941 Professor of Sociology and Public Affairs at Princeton University. The Dean's Fund for Faculty Research in the Woodrow Wilson School provided vital support we needed to develop this project. The National Science Foundation awarded a graduate fellowship to Rourke O'Brien, which made it possible for him to devote time to this book.

To all these friends, colleagues, and institutions we offer our gratitude for ideas, support, and the willingness to debate the impact of the nation's tax policies on our most vulnerable citizens.

CHAPTER ONE

The Evolution of Southern Tax Structures

In the state of Alabama today, one of the most important sources of revenue for state and local governments is a tax that can be as high as 12 percent on food for home consumption. Those who can least afford it face a heavy burden for the very staff of life. Food taxes push poor people in exactly the direction they should avoid at all costs: low quality but inexpensive diets that increase obesity and imperil their health. How did Alabama come to rely on such a regressive tax policy? Why do the other states of the old Confederacy look so much like Alabama?

In their important article comparing the development of the French and American systems of federal taxation, Morgan and Prasad argue that the United States relied on relatively progressive systems of income tax and rejected the use of regressive sales taxes, while the French moved in the opposite direction.[1] At the federal level this is true. But when we look one notch below, we find that many states, particularly those in the South, took the opposite tack and ended up looking far more like the French than we might have expected.

To the rich historical literature on the fiscal dilemmas of the nineteenth century and the Jim Crow era we add an original analysis of trends in state tax revenues over time. Together, these accounts paint a picture of a punishing regime affecting the poor of the South but never imposed on their counterparts in the northern and midwestern states. This historical legacy forms the backdrop for contemporary patterns of southern poverty, which are deeper and significantly more persistent than in other regions of the country.

TAX POLICY BEFORE THE CIVIL WAR

Although the most relevant periods for our purpose are the Civil War era, the Radical Reconstruction that followed, and the Redemption period that overturned the progressive achievements of Reconstruction, we must actually turn the historical dial back further to understand why the Civil War provoked the changes in tax policy that are so important today. Indeed, we must back up to the colonial era and the pathbreaking scholarship of historian Robin Einhorn, who has given us the most comprehensive understanding of fiscal policy in the early years of our nation. In her book *American Taxation, American Slavery*, Einhorn explains that northern states came into the nineteenth century with fairly mature property tax schemes, established during the colonial and Revolutionary War periods. Southern states, by contrast, had exemptions in place that put most land out of the reach of colonial taxation, and they had slaves—the most valuable property in the South—who were labeled and taxed as "persons" through poll taxes.[2] The systems of property taxation in the South were therefore more underdeveloped and did not take shape in many ways until the antebellum period of 1830–1850.

By that time, class conflicts that set slaveholders and non-slaveholders apart intensified debates over appropriate systems of taxation. As Einhorn outlines in detail,[3] the reapportionment of state legislatures throughout the nineteenth century threatened the influence of slaveholding elites as power shifted to burgeoning inland districts populated largely by non-slaveholding small landowners. As these small farmers "called for legislative reapportionment so that their majority number could be translated to majority power, they had to persuade slaveholding minorities that they would not impose heavy or prohibitive slave taxes."[4]

The result was a spate of "uniformity clauses"[5] that made it illegal to tax chattel more than other kinds of assets. With Maryland, a slave state, having included a uniformity clause in its state constitution in 1776, other slave states followed: Missouri in 1820, Tennessee in 1834, Arkansas in 1836, Florida in 1838, and Louisiana and Texas in 1845.[6] Uniformity clauses had two important consequences. First, with most taxable wealth in the hands of slave owners, uniformity clauses acted as a pressure to hold down tax revenue altogether and set a pattern of low levels of financial support for the common costs of public administration in southern states. Second, the protection of slave owners set in motion efforts to tax others—particularly business owners and professionals—more, uniformity clauses or no. Louisiana added license fees and other kinds of taxes on businesses and particular professions in order to protect landed elites and slave owners. Differentiated rates and underassessment had the same impact. For example, the state of New York had a general property tax: one rule for taxation of all property. Elsewhere this was not the tradition: Mississippi favored landholders with the lowest ad valorem rate and slaveholders with a flat rate that was even lower.

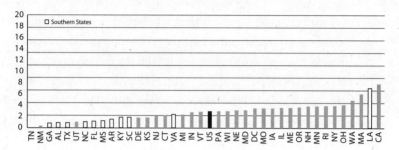

Figure 1. State and local property tax revenue, 1860 (dollars per capita). Per capita calculations are based on states' total populations—slave and free—in 1860. Dollars are 1860 dollars. Source: U.S. Census Bureau, *1870 Decennial Census.*

All in all, as figure 1 suggests, these differences in tax regimes meant that general property tax revenue was very low in most of the southern states, while it made up a considerable proportion of the public resources in the North. Low levels of taxation meant that the resources available to support the development of public institutions (schools, roads, ports, etc.) were far lower in the vast majority of southern states than in their northern counterparts. With the exception of Louisiana, which was a trade center and hence blessed with industry and other forms of property beyond land and slaves, the South entered the Civil War era with a much weaker tax structure for generating revenue and a far less generous tradition of providing for the poor than the rest of the country.

TAX REGIMES DURING THE CIVIL WAR

Financing a war of such huge scope was not an easy matter for either the Union or the Confederacy. Indeed, the genesis of the income tax was to raise federal revenue in the northern states for the pursuit of the Civil War.[7] The Union made use of other devices as well, but as Yale political scientist Rose Razaghian has shown, it was able to fully finance 20 percent of its war costs through taxation, while tax revenue covered only 4 percent of the Confederacy's considerable military expenditures.[8] With continued opposition to the taxation of slaves as property by southern elites, the Confederate States of America (CSA) turned to non-interest-bearing treasury notes and loans to finance the war efforts: a strategy that predictably resulted in hyperinflation. They indulged in "in kind" taxes by confiscating produce and other goods to fuel the army, a particularly harsh burden for poorer white farmers. Nonetheless, these means of raising revenue fell short.

By 1863, Confederate leaders were forced to consider new avenues to finance the war effort. Accordingly, Richmond mimicked the northern strategy by enacting a progressive income tax, a suite of excise and license fees, an 8 percent sales tax on selected goods, and a 10 percent tax on wholesale profits and agricultural products.[9] Here again, though, wealthy slave-owning elites, who controlled the largest landholdings, had the power to ensure favorable treatment—slaves and many valuable forms of property were spared from assessment. These new taxes therefore generated little revenue and failed to ameliorate the worsening financial—and strategic—position of the CSA.

As the momentum of the war shifted in favor of the Union, prominent Confederate policy makers—notably those from states that stood to face the most "economic, social and political upheaval" from emancipation—began to reconsider their dogmatic aversion to taxation.[10] Faced with the reality of an empty treasury and the unsettling prospect that defeat would result in emancipation, the CSA levied a suite of taxes that cut into the pocketbooks of the wealthy. Taxes on property, including slaves (taxed at 5 percent), gold and jewels (taxed at 10 percent), and interest or shares in banks and companies (taxed at 5 percent), were assessed in 1864. The tax on corporate profits was increased to 10 percent, and the CSA even created a windfall tax of 25 percent on all companies that made more than a 25 percent profit.[11] Almost immediately after these new taxes were implemented, they were increased unilaterally by 20 percent, with corporate profits being taxed an additional 30 percent. A $118 million windfall, more than ten times what was in the public coffers for the war under the previous tax structure, followed.

The Civil War created almost unimaginable havoc for civilian populations caught in its maw. For those who were left behind the lines, the spread of poverty and hunger was devastating, nowhere more than in the southern states, where so many of the great battles took place. Even when the campaign favored the southern states in the East, as it did prior to Gettysburg, the mere fact that the battlegrounds were largely on southern territory meant that victory was almost as costly as defeat for civilians. The stuff of daily life—from food to equipment—was requisitioned by the home army.

Ironically, the Civil War spurred progressive efforts to provide for indigent southerners. Direct public aid on a grand scale became available for the first time, reversing a long (and rather miserly) tradition of private charity. According to historian Elna Green, at least one-fourth of the white population of Alabama was receiving state or county assistance in the last few years of the war.[12] Benefits were meager compared to what was available to civilians in the North, but the Confederate government began to provide direct relief, distributing food to the poor for the first time.

The Civil War marked the first time southern states were willing to increase taxes on property for badly needed revenue.

This epiphany, however, came too late to change the course of the war. The defeat of the South led to the quick dissolution of property taxes adopted to fund the war.

THE COST OF RECONSTRUCTION

Eric Foner's classic work on the Reconstruction era transformed our understanding of the period, from the popular conception of carpetbagger incompetence to that of progressive intervention that threw the energies of the state into reversing long-standing inequalities. Initially, however, under the guise of Andrew Johnson's policy of Presidential Reconstruction, state governments in the South were allowed to pursue their own policies without northern interference, and predictably, they leaned heavily toward protecting the interests of white elites. White veterans enjoyed pension programs and homes for veterans and widows, and the war wounded among them received money for artificial limbs.[13]

Once Congress took the lead during Radical Reconstruction, federal agencies, particularly the Freedmen's Bureau, began to tend to the needs of the civilian poor—including the white poor—and the black population newly released from bondage. As Elna Green explains, the Freedmen's Bureau and the U.S. Army launched massive relief programs to prevent starvation in the region.[14] In some of the larger cities they opened soup kitchens, and in other places they experimented with work relief projects of the kind the country would not see again until the New Deal era. These efforts were met with disdain by white landowners, who complained that freedmen would not work so long as free rations were available to them.[15] And local government agencies did what they could to fob off the obligations for one group of paupers onto other jurisdictions. Poor relief was not a popular cause.

Yet the needs of the poor were almost endless. Slavery's demise saw a vast increase in the indigent population, and the cost of addressing their needs mounted quickly. During Radical Reconstruction, the newly formed state legislatures increased drastically the tax bill paid by white property owners to pay for the education of all children, black and white, a practice that outraged small landholders who had traditionally paid very low taxes. The expansion of services went to a population on both sides of the color line that had never been provided for in the slavery period, and the costs were imposed on defeated white elites. But where were the funds to come from? Radical Reconstruction legislators turned to land taxes to increase revenues, and property taxes increased four- to eightfold in the Reconstruction period.[16]

The tax fell upon property holders, but this included very few blacks or poor whites, as they rarely owned much in the way of property. The number of taxpayers stayed roughly constant, while the population they were supposed to support doubled instantly. Inflation in the postwar period also took its toll, requiring an increase in tax rates just to stay even with the revenue demands.

While the southern states remain at the bottom in figure 2, the amount of revenue generated per capita nearly doubled during the Reconstruction period. In 1860, Georgia generated less than $1.00 per capita; by 1870, the rate had doubled in current dollars. Mississippi was at $1.20 per capita in 1860, but ten years later, after the new regime had come to power, the state was up to $4.00 per capita. Similar increases developed in the northern states, but the transformation was more profound in the South,

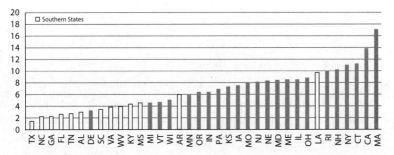

Figure 2. State and local property tax revenue, 1870 (dollars per capita). Dollars are 1870 dollars. Source: U.S. Census Bureau, *1870 Decennial Census.*

with its long tradition of ignoring the welfare needs of its poor, black and white. The increased revenue is even more striking when we consider the sharp decline in the value of property in southern states due to both the ravages of war and the emancipation of slaves, the source of much taxable wealth in the South.

REVERSING COURSE IN THE REDEMPTION ERA

Eric Foner and others have pointed out that if Radical Reconstruction had lasted for fifty years, instead of twelve, we might have seen an entirely different racial history in the United States. Instead, the federal government pulled out of the South and abandoned African Americans to a terrible fate at the hands of oppressive Jim Crow regimes. Histories of the "Redemption" period record the lamentations of black citizens as federal troops disappeared from the region and the old power structure of the white South reasserted control.

Whatever else this reversal implied for those at the bottom of the social structure, it spelled the end of the progressive tax policies that had fueled educational expansion, land reform, and public works investments. White politicians retook southern legislatures in the late 1870s and proceeded to slash state budgets and cut taxes. We can glimpse the up-and-down trajectory of property tax by looking at how the typical tax burden on a 160-acre farm in Mississippi changed over the period from 1848 to 1880, provided by historian J. Mills Thornton III.[17] Before the outbreak of the war, the typical state land tax rate on a farm of this size was only 1.6 mills per acre (table 1). Radical Reconstruction saw that rate jump to 9 mills and climb another 3.5 mills over the succeeding two years. But when the backlash took hold in 1877, the rate dropped back to 5, and later down to 3 mills. What's more, the assessed value of the property was artificially lowered, further reducing the tax burden on landowners. All over the southern states, the same pattern took hold, inflation notwithstanding.

State investment in social welfare services of all kinds dropped precipitously. The tax codes of most southern states reverted to preferential treatment of property, which protected white elites from bearing much of a burden for public sector expenditures. According to historian C. Vann Woodward, "redemption governments, often describing themselves as the 'rule of the taxpayer,' frankly constituted themselves champions of the property owner against the property less and allegedly untaxed masses."[18] In comments published in the Richmond *Dispatch,* celebrated newspaper editor and Democratic congressman Henry Watterson proclaimed, "Intelligence and property must rule over imbecility and pauperism [for this is the] law alike of nature and society."[19] Relative to the rest of the country, property taxes were set very low, and what public monies there were tended to be held inside the boundaries of white communities.

While the rest of the country was pouring money into schooling, per pupil expenditures in the South eroded between 1870

Table 1

State land tax on a farm of 160 acres valued at
the average per acre, Mississippi

Year	Average value per acre (dollars)	Tax rate (mills)	Value (dollars)	Tax (dollars)
1848	3.82	2.5	611.2	1.53
1850	4.54	1.25	726.4	0.91
1852	5.7	1.6	812	1.46
1853	5.67	1.6	907.2	1.45
1854	5.57	1.6	891.2	1.43
1857	6.97	1.6	1,115.2	1.78
1871	4.38	9	700.8	6.31
1872	4.33	8.5	692.8	5.89
1873	4.26	12.5	681.6	8.52
1875	4.01	7.25	641.6	4.65
1876	4.04	6.5	646.4	4.2
1877	4.03	5	644.8	3.22
1878	4.07	3.5	651.2	2.28
1879	2.72	3.5	435.2	1.52
1880	2.76	3	441.6	1.32

NOTE: Shaded years denote property tax increases during Radical
Reconstruction.

SOURCE: J. Mills Thornton III, "Fiscal Policy and the Failure of
Radical Reconstruction in the Lower South," in *Region, Race and
Reconstruction, Essays in Honor of C. Vann Woodward*, ed. J. Morgan
Kousser and James M. McPherson, p. 349–94 (New York: Oxford
University Press, 1982), p. 368.

and 1890. The percentage of the population in southern schools
almost doubled, but the revenue to support their needs was simply not made available.[20] The length of the school year contracted by 20 percent. Under these conditions, it is little wonder
that human capital in the South declined at a rapid rate. Louisiana's illiteracy rate actually increased between 1880 and 1900.[21]

To the extent that southern states were providing for public benefits at all, they placed the heaviest burden of taxation on the poor, who derived the fewest public benefits.[22] Poll taxes and license taxes, fencing laws, restrictions on hunting—all of these mechanisms were put into place by Redemption governments in order to force blacks to go to work for wages rather than engage in self-sufficient farming. Tax policy—as Foner's work makes clear—was part and parcel of a much larger system of legislation that aimed to keep blacks in a state of dependency: stuck in low-wage jobs, unable to vote, consigned to inferior schools (or none at all), and terrorized by lynching.

The state of North Carolina provides an illustrative example of how Redemption era policy makers in the South fought to reverse the progressive tax reforms of the Radical Reconstruction period. As historian J. Morgan Kousser details, under Radical Reconstruction, a uniform, statewide property tax was levied to fund public education in North Carolina, and all revenue generated was to be redistributed equally to finance the education of blacks and whites across the state.[23] As blacks and poor whites owned less property, the tax served to redistribute money from wealthy white communities to the state's blacks and poor whites. A conservative-led revolution in 1870–71 led to the impeachment of the radical governor and removal of the state superintendent. North Carolina's Redeemers set to work reversing the progressive policies of Radical Reconstruction, first by allowing localities to keep the revenues they generated under the property tax, predictably resulting in enormous inequality in per pupil expenditure between wealthy white communities and poorer localities, white and black. Whites pushed for a constitutional amendment "to limit black school expenditures to the amount paid by Negroes in taxes" that ultimately was never codified, in part out of fear such an amendment would generate unwanted attention from the Supreme Court.[24] Even so, the underlying sentiment was clear.[25]

The rollback of progressive taxation—and equitable funding for education—during the Redemption era was hardly unique to North Carolina. Nor was opposition to the practice. Populist movements that came into being specifically to protest unfair taxation proliferated in many states. The Readjuster Party in Virginia was one of the most colorful. Led by attorney Harrison Riddleberger and a former Confederate general, William Mahone, the Readjusters aimed to dismantle the power of wealth and privilege and infuse state resources into public education. Had parties of this kind been victorious, arguably the South would have come out of the nineteenth century looking more like the northern states. Sadly, the black-white coalitions that brought Mahone to power in 1870 fell apart in the early 1880s, giving way to rule by conservative Democrats that lasted for the next eighty years.

Uniformity clauses, originally incorporated into southern state constitutions to limit the power of the majority to tax the elite minority, began to exercise even greater power to restrain taxation in general. Einhorn notes that by the 1880s, judges relied on those statutes to strike down virtually every major reform designed to increase the resources at the disposal of states to feed the public sector.[26] "Income taxes, inheritance taxes, corporation taxes, and taxes at progressive rates" all fell afoul of uniformity clauses: In states without clauses, judges disciplined legislatures and local officials by invoking "implied" uniformity mandates. In the name of equal taxation, the courts held the legislatures in a vise that translated into rock-bottom levels of revenue per capita in the southern tax coffers. As our analysis of the census data shows (figure 3), by 1890 the states of the old Confederacy were unable to generate anything more than an anemic level of property tax revenue to sustain their public infrastructure.

No southern state in 1890 (figure 4) climbed above $6 per capita.

Indeed, southern states had very little revenue to spend on their public sector, period. The lack of revenue translated directly into a poorly funded educational system. Hence the South trailed the rest of the country on public school spending per capita (in the state population; figure 5) and per capita of pupils enrolled.

At precisely the point in American history when the rest of the country was pouring money—and teenagers—into universal high school enrollment, the South lagged behind in all respects. In their important book on education and technology across the twentieth century, Claudia Goldin and Larry Katz point to great advantages the United States reaped from this investment in education as it spread throughout the economy, creating a reservoir of skill that outstripped the rest of the developed world.[27] But the South was way behind. Even if we confine attention to white youth in the period 1850–1880, the rates of high school enrollment in the southern states were drastically lower than in the Northeast or the Midwest.[28] If we add in the black population, the educational profile of the old Confederacy looks far worse. Indeed, as these two economists explain, "youth in most parts of the South had the lowest rates of high school enrollment in the nation."[29]

Hence the South headed for the next watershed moment in American history, the Great Depression, already handicapped by a poorly educated population, divided by race and class, with a weak infrastructure owing to underinvestment by state governments, and above all with a strong tradition of ignoring the needs of the poor. Taxation levels were low and inadequate to the task of

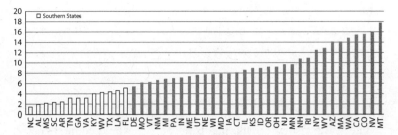

Figure 3. State and local **property tax** revenue, 1890 (dollars per capita). Dollars are 1890 dollars. Source: U.S. Census Bureau, *Statistical Abstract of the United States, 1910.*

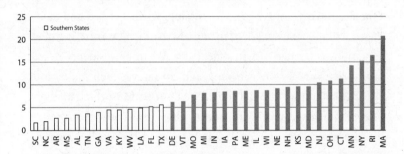

Figure 4. Total state and local **expenditure**, 1890 (dollars per capita). Dollars are 1890 dollars. Source: U.S. Census Bureau, *1890 Decennial Census.*

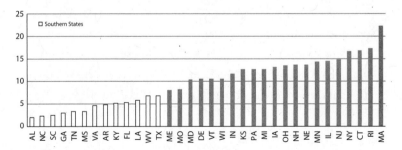

Figure 5. Total state and local **education spending** per pupil, 1890. Source: U.S. Census Bureau, *1890 Decennial Census.*

modern governance.[30] These customs exacerbated the bite of the Depression as the downturns of the early 1930s gathered speed to become an economic calamity of unprecedented proportions.

REJECTING THE NEW DEAL

The 1930s visited terrible hardship on the whole country, but the devastation of the Great Depression was arguably more serious in the rural South than in almost any other region. Prices for cotton, a mainstay of southern agriculture, dropped through the floorboards. In 1927, the Mississippi River flooded and damaged an enormous swath of the fertile river valley, bringing devastation to farmers. Eight out of ten Arkansas residents relied on agriculture for their income, and cotton was their main crop.

Overplanting, and the replacement of cotton (which anchors deeply in the ground) with wheat (which grabs only the surface) in the aftermath of World War I, reduced the land to a dusty plain vulnerable to erosion.[31] The drought that spread through the Midwest, Texas, Oklahoma, and Arkansas exacerbated the problem and led to the infamous Dust Bowl that destroyed the livelihoods of millions of small landholders, spread the devastating "dust pneumonia," and sent thousands onto the highways in search of another place to make a living. These tragedies landed on the backs of farmers long before the stock market collapsed and mass unemployment began to impact the northern industrial cities.

Families accustomed to fending for themselves suddenly discovered they had nothing, and the prospects for jobs that would rescue them evaporated quickly. Poverty spread rapidly and penetrated deeply, especially in rural areas. The only saving grace was the ability of farming families to grow their own food if they still had access to the land, something that was harder for urban dwellers to do. But all across the country, the desperate turned to the government for help in ways that had never been customary before. Private charities that had fended for the poor as best they could were simply unable to meet the demand.[32]

In the northern states, where a history of poor relief was relatively well established, local and state governments expanded their capacity to address the needs of the newly unemployed, and they willingly partnered with President Franklin Delano Roosevelt in New Deal programs that were based on matching funds. In this fashion, the federal government and the northern states erected a safety net that, meager as it was, prevented widespread hunger and eviction and then took to the task of putting millions back to work. The nation did not neglect the South: nearly $2 billion of federal money streamed through the hands of the Federal Emergency Relief Administration (FERA), the Civil Works Administration, and the Works Progress Administration, bound for the southern states.

New Deal policies helped to rescue many poverty-stricken southerners but did so almost in spite of local government, whose insistent refusal to participate in relief efforts that required state or local resources of any kind hurt the down-and-out. As historian Roger Biles explains, "long-standing attitudes regarding self-reliance, limited government and balanced budgets persisted; social welfare matters continued to command a low priority throughout the south."[33] Hence, while state and local governments elsewhere in the country were hemorrhaging red ink in an effort to keep workers on the payroll, southern governments ran surpluses. Southern governments were not so ideologically opposed to the concept of relief that they avoided federal benefits that came without local strings attached. Indeed, as economic historian Gavin Wright has argued, the flow of federal dollars, in the form of Public Works Administration projects for road building, schools, electrification, hospitals, and other essentials, modernized the infrastructure of the South. It literally brought the population of the South into the modern world, since electricity meant that radios could bring the outside world into the living rooms of rural southerners.[34] But when the feds asked southern governors to join the cause with a financial contribution of their own, the answer was usually "no."

Louisville and Little Rock started relief programs but quickly ran out of money, since no funds had been set aside to run them. Houston did not provide any assistance for the unemployed and refused to issue bonds for public works employment. The mayor of Richmond steadfastly refused to seek or accept assistance from the federal government.[35] By 1932, the city of New Orleans was "ranked last among the nation's thirty-one largest metropolitan areas in the amount spent on relief."[36] By 1934, the Big Easy was the largest American city to provide absolutely nothing for family relief, including aid for needy mothers. Only the blind received public assistance in New Orleans.

The state of Georgia was bound by Redemption era amendments to the state constitution that outlawed municipal debts "except to repel invasion, suppress insurrection . . . or to pay existing public debt."[37] The Depression did not qualify, and hence indigent citizens of the Peachtree State went without. Alabama was even harsher. Birmingham passed a budget control law limiting expenditures to the amount of annual income. Similar efforts by policy makers across the South enabled many cities to post surpluses by cutting wages for municipal employees, slashing education funding, and stripping public health programs.[38] The most that mayors did to combat rising unemployment was to put their citizens to work selling produce, launching campaigns to "buy an apple in Memphis" or an orange in New Orleans.[39]

New Deal era southern politicians were particularly hard-hearted when it came to addressing the needs of the unemployed. Harry Hopkins, President Roosevelt's director of FERA, worked overtime to involve southern officials in the distribution of emergency relief. Congress had mandated that the states contribute to FERA's operations, but Hopkins met a stone wall in the region, and the federal government ended up footing most of the bill. While a significant flow of federal funds went south, it was a weaker stream than it should have been. In the 1930s, the South had one-quarter of the nation's population, but by 1939 it had garnered only one-sixth of the expenditures of FERA, the Civil Works Administration, and the Works Progress Administration.[40]

To the extent that the South responded to the needs of the poor (and the public sector more generally), it led the way in the use of regressive taxes to fund the expenditures. Property values fell dramatically throughout the Depression all over the country, and many households simply could not afford the tax bill. Over time, revenues derived from this source became less and less useful as an income generator for states. Sociologist Isaac Martin has argued that the first great property tax revolt owes itself to precisely this implosion in property values. The practice of copying the same assessed value on property year after year laid the groundwork for a crisis in the 1930s. As prices for homes and farms tumbled, tax bills remained constant while the values of these assets tanked. Property owners protested by supporting legislation that placed limits on state and local property taxes and parallel lids on spending.

Not surprisingly, over time, revenues derived from property

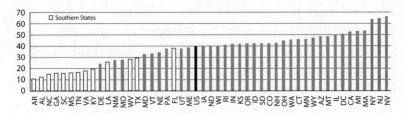

Figure 6. State and local property tax revenue, 1932 (dollars per capita). Dollars are 1932 dollars. Source: U.S. Census Bureau, *1935 Historical Abstract of the United States*.

tax became less and less useful as an income generator for state and local governments everywhere. As figure 6 indicates, the southern states rested at the very bottom of the national barrel in terms of what their property tax revenues brought into the coffers of government. This was not simply a matter of being property poor, for other low-wealth states, notably plains states like Kansas and Nebraska, were able to generate considerably more. Southern states were deliberately underperforming relative to what was fiscally possible, because they were looking to hold public sector expenditures down. If this was intended as a balanced-budget approach to curing the Depression, it worked poorly. Instead, transients swarmed the southern cities and were turned away, since, by design, there were no funds to provide for them.

THE EMERGENCE OF THE SALES TAX

Ironically, it was state debt for construction projects launched in the glory days of the 1920s that pushed some southern governors to seek additional tax revenues in the 1930s, despite generic political resistance to taxation. Mississippi was $14 million in the hole; Arkansas had the highest per capita debt in the country.[41] How were these debts to be cured? In some states, Mississippi included, raising property taxes was constitutionally possible but politically inconceivable, and that was that. Racially inspired voting rights restrictions meant that the very people most likely to favor increases in property taxes could not exercise any influence. Sales tax seemed the ideal solution to those who could vote. It appealed to property owners, who did not want to see their burden increased, and its advocates believed it would be a means of exacting taxes out of African Americans who had little property to be taxed in the first place.[42]

In 1932, Mississippi adopted a 2 percent general sales tax, becoming the first state to opt for this form of regressive taxation as a source of revenue. When the state tax was upheld by the Mississippi senate in 1934, a headline in the *Atlanta Constitution* read, "House Passes Bill to Insure Relief for Property Tax Payers."[43] Similarly, in Oklahoma, the strongest supporters of the sales tax were property owners who wanted to lower their own taxes.[44] In rapid succession, a series of copycat statutes passed in Kentucky, North Carolina, and Oklahoma. In 1933, North Carolina enacted a retail sales tax of 3 percent,[45] the highest in the nation. Not surprisingly, given the political origins of the sales tax movement, local property taxes began to drop. Between 1930 and 1932, property tax declined 20 percent.[46] Non-southern states also took notice, using sales tax revenue in part to meet the state matching requirements for federal assistance from FERA. Overall, two dozen states—across the South and beyond—adopted sales taxes as a solution to their budget problems during the decade between 1930 and 1940, a move that placed particularly onerous burdens on the poor.

Class politics ignited in response to regressive taxation. Senator Huey Long of Louisiana, one of the principal advocates of wealth redistribution, burnished his populist credentials by insisting that taxing the oil companies was the best way to pay for roads, free textbooks, and public hospitals. Senator Long denounced the sales tax as an attempt on the part of the wealthy to escape their proper share of the cost of government and to shift it to the less fortunate. Long called the tax "rotten all through."[47] The Kingfish was joined by southern New Dealers—politicians like Governor Olin D. Johnston of South Carolina and Senators Claude Pepper of Florida and Al Gore, Sr., of Tennessee—in opposing the sales tax and agitating for more-progressive forms of revenue raising. However, southern New Dealers were usually outnumbered or blocked by state supermajority requirements and other political barriers.

African Americans also insisted that this new mechanism for raising money was a fiscal calamity for their community. An editorial in the *New Journal and Guide,* an African-American newspaper, criticized the sales tax for shifting burdens from the rich to the poor. "The rich man, the large real estate owner ... now wants the average man to pay his (the rich man's) taxes when he buys his sugar and coffee and shoes and coal," the editorial railed, "since he can no longer collect rents on the basis of what the City and State figure his investment in real estate to be worth." The opinion page concludes that the "*Journal and Guide* is opposed to a retail sales tax because it adds further to the burden of the poor."[48] The rapid spread of the sales tax led some at the time to label it "an emergency tax"[49]—yet the emergency became permanent. Over the next few decades, many progressive states tried to lessen the regressive nature of the tax by excluding basic necessities such as food and medicine.[50] Most of the southern states never got that far. Instead, the exigencies of the Great Depression laid the groundwork for reliance on consumption taxes (table 2) for state and local services—especially education—that continues to this day.[51]

Table 2
Inauguration of general state sales taxes

1932–33	1934–35	1936–38
Mississippi (1932)	Missouri (1934)	Alabama (1936)
North Carolina (1933)	Ohio (1934)	Kansas (1937)
Oklahoma (1933)	North Dakota (1935)	Louisiana (1938)
West Virginia (1933)	Colorado (1935)	
Arizona (1933)	Hawaii (1935)	
California (1933)	Wyoming (1935)	
New Mexico (1933)	Arkansas (1935)	
Utah (1933)		
Washington (1933)		
Illinois (1933)		
Indiana (1933)		
Iowa (1933)		
Michigan (1933)		
South Dakota (1933)		

SOURCE: Advisory Commission on Intergovernmental Relations, *Significant Features of Fiscal Federalism*, vol. 1 (Washington, DC: U.S. Government Printing Office, 1994), p. 34.

SOCIAL INSURANCE

The lasting legacy of the New Deal for most Americans lies in the Social Security system.[52] As Ira Katznelson has shown,[53] southern antipathy for the progressive consequences of this program was relentless. Hailed virtually everywhere else, the centerpiece of the New Deal was perceived as an attack on southern structures of racial subordination and an intrusion into the labor market arrangements that bound black workers to paternalistic employers.

The original bill enjoined the states from imposing any conditions for the receipt of old age assistance and required that state pensions, when added to the recipient's income, furnish "a reasonable subsistence compatible with decency and health."[54] Both provisions were stripped from the bill that emerged from the House Ways and Means Committee. Accordingly, states could impose any conditions they saw fit, and the subsistence provision was eliminated entirely, enabling states to pay pensions that were as small as they desired. Southern congressmen campaigned to exclude domestic and agricultural workers from Social Security,[55] on pain of exercising a block veto unless they got their way. Over two-thirds of the black labor force was concentrated in domestic service and sharecropping in the 1930s.

Old age insurance was not the only target of southern ire. The Aid to Dependent Children (ADC) program, designed to assist widows with the cost of raising their children, and the Old Age Assistance program, which provided welfare to the aged poor, were brought under local control—the price for southern acquiescence to the Social Security Act. Originally, states were to be required to pay ADC and Old Age Assistance benefits that would permit a decent standard of living. Once again, the requirement was eliminated because of "objection to Federal determination of adequacy on the part of Southern members who feared Northern standards would be forced on the South in providing for Negro and White tenant families."[56] Decision-making power was instead left in the hands of state and local administrators. Southern members of Ways and Means even inserted a provision into the act that set an upper limit on the amount of federal assistance provided to the state.

The southern assault on the ADC program during the New Deal has had lasting implications for regional inequalities in welfare support through Aid to Families with Dependent Children (AFDC) and, since 1996, Temporary Assistance for Needy Families (TANF)—the lineal descendants of ADC. Southern states continue to provide the most meager levels of cash assistance of any states in the Union: South Carolina, Alabama, Arkansas, and Mississippi, for example, currently provide only one-fourth to one-fifth of the assistance level of the New England states.[57]

The combination of dependence on regressive consumption taxes to raise revenue and politically inspired limits on eligibility and benefit levels for federal programs of old age assistance and child welfare set up a toxic fiscal environment for the poor in the South.

POSTWAR TAX REGIMES

Since the end of the Great Depression, it has become an article of faith that government bears important responsibilities for the care of the poor, although the able-bodied poor are often less welcome within the social contract. Less controversial is the requirement that government provide for the free education of all children at a reasonable level of quality (a provision generally enshrined in state constitutions). Neither of these assumptions came easily to the South.

In the postwar period, most states surrendered property taxes to local governments to be used, in the main, for the support of education. Southern states, however, were unable to generate as much revenue from property tax as other states, as figure 7 makes clear.[58]

Indeed, if anything, the gap between southern states and the rest of the country in terms of the revenues generated by property tax got worse over time (figure 8).

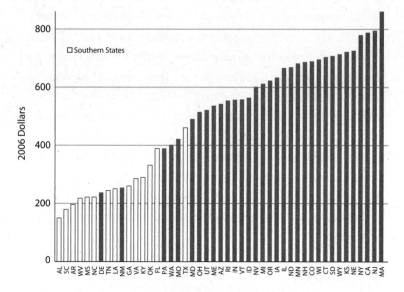

Figure 7. State and local property tax revenue per capita, 1957. Dollars are 1957 dollars. Source: U.S. Census Bureau, *1957 Census of Governments.*

At the same time, many southern states slashed their corporate income taxes. Before World War II, southern states employed a corporate income tax that, on average, was the highest of any region in the country, the product of landholding elites shifting the tax burden to industry. After the war, state politicians leaned on the tax code to create incentives for business to move south. This about-face was accomplished by slashing corporate taxes. Historian Gavin Wright notes, "Between 1950 and 1978, the median corporate tax rate in the South went from 85 percent above, to 13 percent below, that of the rest of the country."[59] Lower taxes coupled with cheap labor lured industry to the Sunbelt, sparking tremendous economic growth in the latter half of the twentieth century.[60] Despite increased economic activity,

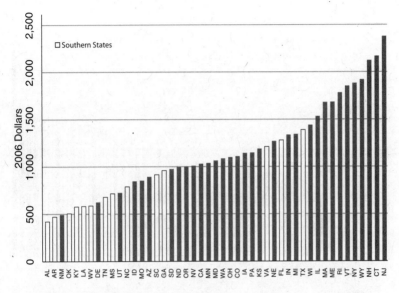

Figure 8. State and local property tax revenue per capita, 2006. Source: U.S. Census Bureau, *2007 Census of Governments.*

corporate income tax rates were set too low to fill the coffers of state treasuries.

It must be said that the move to create a favorable business climate by limiting corporate taxes helped to ensure that the South would have lower unemployment rates, by far, than the industrial region of the North as deindustrialization gripped the Rust Belt. The South had, and has today, largely a low-wage economy, but there is no denying that unique among the regions, the poverty rate came down from a high in the 1960s that was well above the rest of the country. In 1969, the first year for which the census provides poverty data across the regions, the South weighed in at 17.9 percent, nearly double the rate in the Midwest. By 2008, the South had a poverty rate of 14.3 percent, which was

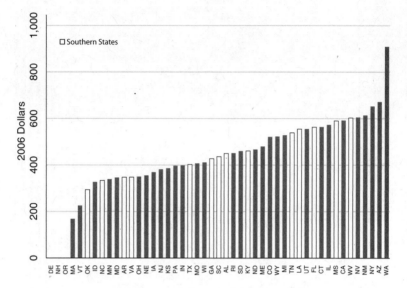

Figure 9. State and local general sales tax revenue per capita, 1972. No data for Delaware, New Hampshire, and Oregon because they did not generate money from sales tax. Source: U.S. Census Bureau, *1972 Census of Governments.*

higher than the Midwest (at 12.4 percent) but significantly lower than it had been in the late 1960s, while the Midwest had moved in the opposite direction.[61] Arguably, as an economic development strategy in the midst of globalization pressures that off-shored manufacturing jobs by the millions, the southern "low road" worked, if by *worked* we mean it attracted firms and provided jobs to southern citizens at rock-bottom wage rates. A low-wage economy will not support the public sector, since the population is earning little. Where, then, does the South turn to fill the coffers? To the sales tax.

Whereas southern states are at the bottom in property tax revenues, the relationship changes when we consider sales taxes, as figure 9 indicates. There the southern states are closer to

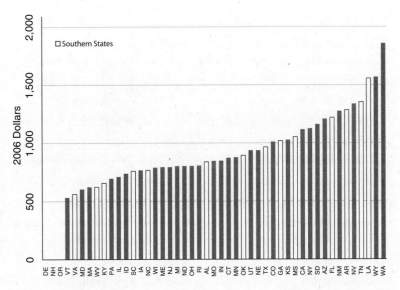

Figure 10. State and local general sales tax revenue per capita, 2006. No data for Delaware, New Hampshire, and Oregon because they did not generate money from sales tax. Source: U.S. Census Bureau, *2007 Census of Governments.*

the top of the chart, generating far more money from the most regressive taxes than the rest of the country.

The burden continues to exact a toll on the southern poor to this day, as figure 10 makes clear. In 2006, the southern states generated more revenue per capita from sales taxes than did the vast majority of northeastern states, particularly when the absence of adjustments (like those available to New York taxpayers) is taken into account.

CONCLUSION

The history of taxation in the United States is—until the 1970s—a tale of two regions, the South and the rest. The long reach of slavery and the class politics of the "peculiar institution" catalyzed a series of policy adjustments that culminated in far greater reliance on regressive sales taxes than we see in other regions of the country. This is not a technical matter: it is a history with teeth, for the reliance on sales taxes took money from the hands of those who had the least and pushed them deeper into poverty.

Yet starting in the "age of inequality," the period roughly corresponding to the mid-1970s to the present, the western states began moving in the direction of the South. While the West has never soaked the poor as egregiously as the South in terms of tax policy, increasingly it too is funding the public sector through sales taxes that hit the poor harder than anyone else. Arguably, similar consequences are visible there as well: public schools struggling to keep their heads above water, rising user fees to replace revenue lost by declining property tax, and increasingly high rates of pernicious poverty-related outcomes.

CHAPTER TWO

Barriers to Change

Inertia, Supermajorities, and Constitutional Amendments

The legacy of the past—southern opposition to property taxation in the nineteenth century—continues to define the disparities in tax structure and revenue we experience today. Inertia alone leads to the persistence of an underfunded public sector. Politicians are limited in their ability to implement marginal increases in taxes; therefore states starting with the lowest levels of taxation remain at the bottom. But this is not the only way the past haunts the present. Powerful statutory limitations intervene to make it exceptionally hard to change the situation.

Proposition 13, the notorious Jarvis-Gann amendment that rolled back property taxes in California, left a lasting legacy by setting a high bar for any future tax increase. Supermajority rules require a two-thirds vote in the California legislature to increase state taxes. Proposition 13 was considered an innovation—for better or worse—in its own time. In truth, the southern states beat it to the punch decades earlier.

At the height of the Great Depression, when most states were scrambling to generate revenue to assist an increasingly unemployed and impoverished citizenry, residents of Arkansas made it procedurally more difficult to increase taxes in the state. The nineteenth amendment to the state constitution, approved by voters in the general election of November 6, 1934, established for the first time that any subsequent tax increases could be authorized only by a supermajority in the state legislature.[1] Under this new law, any bill that sought to increase existing tax rates had to be approved by a full three-fourths of the state house and senate, as opposed to a traditional simple majority vote.

This procedural hurdle has had lasting consequences in Arkansas. Following the adoption of the amendment, the state supreme court ruled that the supermajority requirement applied only to taxes that were already in existence when the amendment was passed (in 1934), including the property tax, personal and corporate income taxes, and excise taxes on beer and cigarettes. Taxes levied after 1934, including the state sales tax, which was formally adopted in 1941, were therefore exempt from the supermajority requirement. It is no surprise, then, that increasing the sales tax has been the most popular goal of politicians looking for an expedient way to generate new revenue. In the last six decades, the sales tax rate in Arkansas has been increased multiple times, from 2 percent statewide to a state plus local rate as high as 11.5 percent in some jurisdictions.[2]

For more than thirty years, Arkansas remained the only state in the union with a supermajority requirement.[3] That changed in the 1960s. With the civil rights movement promising to forever alter the social and political structure of the South, elites looked for ways to hedge against the tidal wave of change. Following passage of the Voting Rights Act of 1965, which made it clear that black enfranchisement could shift the future balance of power in state legislatures, southern states adopted supermajority requirements in an effort to block future tax increases.[4] Louisiana was first, adopting a constitutional amendment in 1966 that required a two-thirds majority to increase, amend, or appeal any tax in the state. Mississippi followed in 1970 with a constitutional amendment requiring a three-fifths majority for the approval of any revenue or taxation bill in the state legislature. Florida followed in 1971 with the adoption of a constitutional amendment requiring a three-fifths supermajority to increase the corporate income tax in the state above the 5 percent constitutionally defined threshold.

By the late 1970s the supermajority requirement was exported out of the South, with South Dakota and Delaware following suit. Another wave of citizen activism put muscle behind supermajority campaigns in the 1990s, with states such as Washington, Nevada, and Oklahoma adopting their own rules. Today at least sixteen states have adopted some type of supermajority requirement to raise taxes. In addition to the pioneering antitax states of Arkansas, Louisiana, Mississippi, and Florida, the states of Kentucky, Missouri, and Oklahoma have adopted constitutional supermajority requirements.[5]

CONSTITUTIONAL LIMITS ON TAXATION: EVOLUTION OF THE PROPERTY TAX IN ALABAMA

In addition to the supermajority requirements that permit increases in taxation but create high thresholds for approval, a second strategy for limiting taxes was invented that worked by erecting procedural hurdles (rather than legislative voting rules) that made tax increases exceedingly unlikely. This policy spread throughout the South, starting in Alabama in 1875 but spreading quickly to neighboring states, including Texas (1876), Arkansas

(1883), Georgia (1890), and Kentucky (1908).[6] These dates should ring a bell, for they coincide with the Jim Crow era. Between supermajority rules and limits on taxation, the South locked in a low-property-tax environment that led eventually to reliance on other revenue devices, principally the sales tax.

The evolution of the property tax in Alabama provides a case study in both the use of political instruments to shift the tax burden to those at the bottom and the consequences it can have decades later.[7] In 1981, John F. Knight, Jr., Alease S. Sims, et al. filed a lawsuit against the state of Alabama in an effort to eliminate "vestiges of historical, state-enforced, racial segregation and other forms of official racial discrimination against African-Americans in Alabama's system of public universities."[8] After more than twenty-six years of litigation, the case was officially settled in 2007. Public universities in the state agreed to implement "strategic diversity plans" designed to increase the representation of African Americans among the faculty and administration.[9] Their successful litigation strategy was predicated on demonstrating that the current property tax system in the state of Alabama, which is the primary source of funds for education, is traceable to a de jure system of discrimination.

By detailing how the current property tax system evolved from statutes enacted with explicitly racist and inequitable intentions, the plaintiffs attempted to make the case for a complete reform of the system and, thereafter, the fundamentals of education funding in Alabama. The case required the preparation of a detailed history of the Alabama tax system, and this provides us with a clear picture of how constitutional limitations on property tax led directly to reliance on regressive sales tax to fund education.[10]

For much of the period between the state's founding in 1819 and the beginning of the Civil War, the state of Alabama had no formal public school system; the state constitution simply "encouraged" education while giving the legislature the authority to generate revenue for both kindergarten through twelfth grade and higher education. On February 14, 1854, the state legislature established a statewide public school system by giving counties the authority to levy a tax on real and personal property without having to seek voter approval through a referendum. The public school system was reserved exclusively for whites and throughout the Civil War was funded almost exclusively by local taxation.

The immediate postbellum years were a period of tremendous transformation in Alabama. The Radical Reconstruction constitution of 1867 made education a priority and centralized its provision through a statewide public school system. The constitution also increased available revenue to fund public education and authorized local school districts to levy their own poll taxes to supplement state funds. Before the Civil War, slaves were viewed as property and were counted as such in the levying of property taxes on their owners. Emancipation resulted in a dramatic decline in the assessed wealth or property holdings of white landowners in the South; prewar tax rates thus failed to generate sufficient tax revenue after the war. The constitution of 1867 established a state ad valorem property tax that included a uniformity clause whereby all property, including but not limited to land, was subject to taxation. This new property tax, combined with an aggressive enforcement of assessed values by Republican officials, resulted in a dramatic increase in revenues for state public schools, a doubling from the antebellum period to $500,000 per annum.

It was not enough. Since, for the first time in Alabama's history, blacks (and poor whites) were permitted to attend public schools, the population that had to be served with these funds mushroomed. What's more, while schools were segregated from the start, the state board of education mandated that state funds had to be distributed in a way that was proportional to the number of students enrolled, regardless of race. This experiment in racial equality was short-lived.

Radical Reconstruction saw white landholders hit by a steep rise in their tax bills while enjoying no commensurate increase in public services—their money was going to fund the education of blacks, who were largely untouched by the new property taxes since they owned very little real or personal property. White Democrats fought their way back to power during the Redemption period and in 1875 convened a constitutional convention for the explicit purpose of reducing their own tax burden and guarding against the efforts of potential future black majorities to increase taxes on property. They triumphed: the Alabama state constitution of 1875 set strict limits on the property taxes that could be levied by state and local governments. It bears reinforcing that this is not a supermajority provision but rather an out-and-out bar on raising the rates, as historians have explained in expert testimony:

> During Reconstruction, the experience of [Black Belt] whites had been a county government which was controlled by blacks and their Republican allies and which had very heavily taxed them, and taxed them for purposes that they largely regarded as illegitimate, such as the education of the Freedmen. Now that they had power back into their own hands, they were intent on . . . using that new control to protect themselves from the possibility that the black majority in their counties would ever again be able to use that political power . . . to tax them in a way that would force them as the property holders to cough up the funds, . . . which would be used to the benefit of the majority of the people in the Black Belt who were black and essentially non-property holding. . . . And so they wanted to write into the Constitution permanent protections.[11]

The new constitution placed draconian limitations on state education funding: no more than one-fifth of all state revenues could be devoted to the purpose. It did not take long for the effect to be felt: in the first year under the 1875 constitution, education revenue plunged by one-third. Rules requiring that funds be allocated without regard to race were overturned soon after, with the apportionment act of 1891 authorizing local school boards to distribute funds at their discretion. Predictably, dollars drained away from black schools and flowed to the white ones.

Motivated partly by fear that black majorities would regain political power, overturn the Redemption constitution of 1875, and reinstate high property taxes, urban industrialists and white small landholders from the Black Belt convened a convention to draft a new constitution that would disenfranchise blacks. The Alabama state constitution of 1901 codified the limitations on state and local property taxation set forth in 1875, with two changes: First, the new state constitution actually *lowered* the maximum property tax that could be levied by the state (from 7.5 mills to 6.5 mills). Second, the new constitution allowed counties the option to levy an additional 1.0 mill property tax for schools, provided they sought the approval of voters via a *state-wide* referendum. This was the first time a procedural obstacle—as opposed to a voting rule—was placed in the Alabama state constitution for the explicit purpose of limiting the government's future ability to raise taxation. As Wayne Flint notes in his history of Alabama in the twentieth century: "It was the intent of the 1901 framers that government have a difficult or impossible task taxing property. . . . Virtually all Alabama's twentieth-century problems were somehow related to the state's tax structure." The Brookings Institution concluded in 1932 that the taxing authority of the 1901 constitution "warped and distorted" revenue production and created a "gravely defective budgetary system. . . . By 1940 more than 75 percent of the state's tax revenue came from sales or other direct taxes on individuals."[12]

With the same constitutional document virtually ensuring the disenfranchisement of blacks, white voters were then in charge of deciding how citizens would be taxed to pay for schools. Between the racial disenfranchisement and the limitations on property tax, the Jim Crow constitution meant that Alabama would labor under an underfunded, inadequate public school system.[13] This much was understood as long ago as 1919, when State Superintendent Spright Dowell remarked, "Under the present constitution, and in fact, since the Constitution of 1875, we have found ourselves more limited and restricted in the matter of local school support than any state in the Union."[14]

The Great Depression did not improve matters. In 1933, with already low property tax levies generating even less in revenue, the state instituted an income tax by way of constitutional amendment. Funds from the income tax, however, were not immediately allocated to schools. The funds were first used to pay down the state's floating debt and then applied toward a long-term *reduction* in the state property tax. The desperate situation of the schools was addressed only in 1935 and through the most regressive of institutions: the state's first sales tax to provide minimum funding for schools.

This experiment quickly became a habit. Hence even governors who were inclined to support education found themselves unable to rely on any other instrument for raising revenue. After a series of proposals to reform the property tax system to generate more revenue were rejected in the 1950s, the Alabama Education Commission advocated a sales tax increase. According to the historians' testimony, "this tax had long been supported by the Black Belt planters and urban industrialists as a way to ensure that non–property owners of Alabama paid their "'fair share' of the tax burden."[15]

Efforts in the 1950s and 1960s to amend the constitution and increase property taxation failed in the face of staunch opposition from white planters in the Black Belt and urban industrialists, who continued to oppose any increase in the property tax. In 1962, then Governor Patterson did succeed in passing a constitutional amendment permitting localities to raise property taxes by 5 mills, with approval of the voters. In practice, only three cities and eight counties were able to generate the political will to increase local taxes. As the civil rights movement foreshadowed increasing black political power, white property owners intensified their resistance to property taxation. Constitutional amendments adopted in 1971 and 1978 allowed the state to circumvent rulings from federal courts that called for fair assessment and taxation of property, allowing Alabama to preserve the status quo.[16]

What does this mean for taxation and education funding in Alabama today? According to Susan Pace Hamill, professor of law at the University of Alabama and an expert on state tax policy, "The nationwide average of property tax collections per capita imposed at the state, county, municipal, and school district levels, exceeded Alabama's per capita property tax collections by more than three times."[17] Whereas property taxes amount to an average of *one-fourth* of all state and local revenues nationally, in Alabama the property tax contributes only *one-twentieth* of state and local revenue. This underutilization of the property tax, she argues, can help to explain the state's reliance on an overly regressive system of sales taxation to fund vital services such as education, including the peculiarly high sales tax rates imposed by localities within the state. Substituting sales taxes for property taxes does not simply increase tax regressivity, Hamill notes; it also generates less revenue, since low-income communities are unlikely to have the commercial tax base necessary to generate sufficient revenue.[18]

The taxation system in Alabama is marked by extremes: the state and its localities generate the lowest revenue from property taxation of any state while at the same time maintaining the highest sales tax rate in the United States, with some localities posting rates as high as 12 percent, even on basic necessities such as food. The evolution of Alabama's perverse tax structure is a direct result of the limits on taxation codified in the state constitution of 1901. The story was repeated, in most of its particulars, across most of the southern states.

While it is difficult to distill the real effect of supermajority requirements on taxation, recent empirical studies suggest supermajority requirements reduce both the overall level of taxation and public welfare expenditure at the state level. One study by economist Brian Knight finds that even for states with a "pro-tax" party in control of the legislature, adoption of a supermajority requirement decreases the relative tax rate by somewhere between 8 percent and 23 percent.[19] Other scholars argue that these hurdles do not impact taxation but are associated with less spending on redistributive welfare programs.[20]

SHIFTING BURDENS: HOW SUPERMAJORITIES TRANSFORM THE MIX OF TAX REVENUES

The politics of constitutional spending limits and supermajority rules in the Redemption era resurfaced in southern states as the civil rights movement gathered force. Florida, Louisiana, Virginia, and North and South Carolina all introduced constitutional limitations on property taxes and expenditures in the 1960s and

1970s.[21] How well did the strategy work? Our case study of Alabama suggests that it was an effective block on any meaningful increases in more-progressive taxes (particularly property tax) throughout the region.

Did it work elsewhere? Here we zoom out to the nation as a whole and consider the regional divergence in sources of state and local revenue in the period of 1957–2006. We argue that the South remains an outlier, with persistently heavy reliance on regressive sales taxes throughout those fifty years. But as we move closer to the present, the West joins the South in ratcheting up consumption taxes until—today—the two regions look alike in many respects. With property tax increases off limits, and a reluctance to open up debates over the income tax, there were few other alternatives in the South or the West to increasing sales tax.

Figure 11 compares the sources of state and local tax revenue in four regions as they appeared in 1957. In none of these regions were individual or corporate income taxes playing a significant role. The trade-offs were coming from differential reliance on property tax and sales tax, which in this series of figures includes general sales tax revenue, the major "sin" taxes (alcohol, tobacco, pari-mutuel gaming), and special taxes levied on gasoline, public utility usage, and insurance. The Northeast and the Midwest stand out for their heavy reliance on property tax in the late fifties, especially in contrast to the South. The West balances the two.

The balance of property tax and sales tax barely budged in the 1960s. By the end of the 1970s (figure 12), the shape of the future started to become visible. The Northeast remained more reliant on property tax, and the South maintained its persistent reliance on sales tax. But the Midwest saw a significant decline in tax revenues from property tax, and sales taxes moved up in

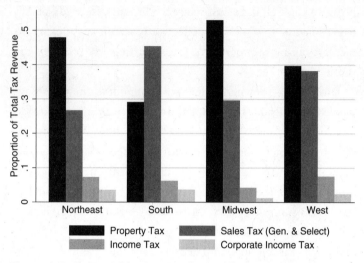

Figure 11. Total state and local tax revenue by source, 1957. Source: U.S. Census Bureau, *1957 Census of Governments.*

the West. The evolution of revenue-raising in the Midwest probably reflected the bite that deindustrialization was beginning to take out of the Midwest as factory flight gathered force, union density declined, and wages began their long descent from the old, historic highs of the industrial heyday toward their contemporary trough. It is in this same period that the West started to mimic the South in shifting toward sales tax. It is a pattern that accelerated with greater force after the passage of Proposition 13 in 1978, which rolled back property tax and put the clamps on future increase through supermajority provisions that have proved durable and insurmountable.

The Permanent Tax Revolt: How the Property Tax Transformed American Politics provides the most thorough and engaging account of the origins of this earth-shaking initiative. Because California home owners faced sharp escalations in the value of their real

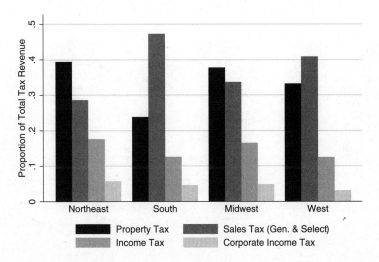

Figure 12. Total state and local tax revenue by source, 1977. Source: U.S. Census Bureau, *1977 Census of Governments*.

estate holdings, they were under the thumb of market forces that seemed uncontrollable. The modernization of assessment practices linked the market price more closely to the tax bill delivered to home-owning voters than had been true in the Depression era. "When reassessment came at long last," author Isaac Martin explains, "homeowners experienced it as a violation of their customary social rights. Fractional assessment had subsidized homeownership; reassessment cut the subsidy."[22]

The hit to taxpayer pocketbooks was grist for the mill of both the Right and the Left. Conservatives considered property tax to be a drag on upstanding citizens who had "worked hard and saved money. From the left, others complained that it was regressive and that poor communities had to charge high tax rates to pay for the same public services that wealthy communities could get more cheaply."[23] Into this perfect political storm marched Jar-

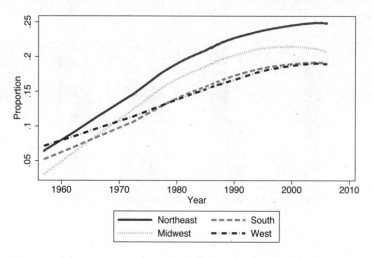

Figure 13. Income tax as a proportion of the total taxes by region, 1957–2006.

vis, Gann, and their political hero: Richard Nixon. Ironically, the president sought an end to property tax for reasons civil rights advocates could love: it lead to unequal schools, based on a community's ability to pay. To be sure, it did not escape his attention that this was an issue dear to the hearts of the antitax movement sweeping the West and, then, the rest.

At the same time, all of the regions began to ratchet up the take from individual income tax, and they did so in a fairly uniform fashion. Of course, the amounts they derived from this source varied tremendously with the wealth of the region and the rate of the tax levies. And the distribution of that burden differed dramatically from one state to the next, with the poor paying a good deal more of the income tax in Mississippi (where poor families are taxed) than in California or New York. But the usage of state income tax, which was negligible in 1957, became more pronounced as the country moved toward the present (figure 13).

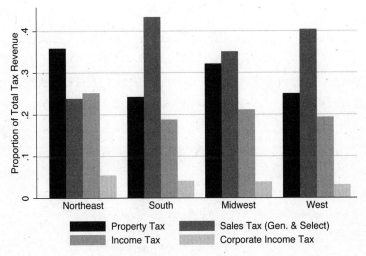

Figure 14. Total state and local tax revenue by source, 2006. Source: U.S. Census Bureau, *2007 Census of Governments*.

By now, the resemblance between the South and the West—where regressive sales tax represents the dominant source of state and local revenue—has been well established (figure 14). This pattern is business as usual in the South, but it is a departure in a regressive direction for the West.

How might we explain the convergence of the western region with the South? Though California has had its share of Republican governors and the South has had its liberal Democrats, we often think of these two regions as culturally distinct. Even in political terms, an Arnold Schwarzenegger—Republican though he may be—would probably never fly in Mississippi. What the two regions appear to share, among other traits, is a penchant for supermajority rules (table 3) that hold back property tax and leave income and sales tax open as a revenue-raising device.

As we noted earlier, income tax has been rising across all four regions. Because the South is a poor part of the country, it

Table 3

States with supermajority requirements

South	West	Other
Arkansas (1934)	California (1979)	South Dakota (1978)
Louisiana (1966)	Colorado (1990)	Delaware (1980)
Mississippi (1970)	Arizona (1992)	
Florida (1971)	Washington (1993)	
Oklahoma (1992)	Nevada (1996)	
	Oregon (1996)	

SOURCE: Brian G. Knight, "Supermajority Voting Requirements for Tax Increases: Evidence from the States," *Journal of Public Economics* 76 (2000): 41–67.

doesn't yield very much (relative to a rich state like New York or Massachusetts). This creates additional pressure to raise revenue from the sources that are available, and in both the West and the South, that is increasingly translating into sales tax, since both regions are saddled with supermajority provisions.

We have argued that the origin of those requirements was linked to fear in the South of rising political power among blacks. The consequence, however, was to set the stage for increasing reliance on sales taxes in the South. Can we make the same argument for the West? Some economists and political scientists have argued that racial and ethnic diversity leads to a reduced willingness to pay taxes, since the beneficiaries are less likely to look like the majority.[24] Whether this was an important dynamic in the passage of Proposition 13 is debatable. There is no rhetoric in the Proposition 13 campaign that points to minority needs for public services as a motivation for tax revolts.

The Immigration and Nationality Act of 1965 opened the

door to family reunification through immigration and led to a sharp upswing in Mexican migration, especially to California. It is conceivable that fourteen years later a similar logic about blocking tax increases to support the increasing burdens on the public sector prevailed. Anger over affirmative action was certainly at its height in the Golden State then, and it raised the temperature of white attitudes toward minorities. Proposition 13 also stoked more general conservative politics in California, already primed by the governorship of Ronald Reagan. But there is no real evidence that racial divisions played an important role in gathering support for California's property tax revolt. Martin points out that "hostility to the property tax was pervasive in many other states and the variation in anti–property tax attitudes, behavior, and legislation is well accounted for by variation in property assessment regimes."[25] Californians were genuinely worried about being taxed out of their homes, and Proposition 13 promised to roll back assessments and limit them in various ways going forward. This, and not the composition of the population that would be served by the tax coffers, fueled the initiative.

The history of devolution in the 1960s and 1970s is the more likely culprit in the shift of the West toward reliance on sales taxes. Timothy Conlan's book on intergovernmental reform makes the case that the 1960s saw an enormous expansion of the role of the federal government during the period of Johnson's Great Society.[26] From education at all levels to law enforcement to fire departments, Conlan argues, local control yielded to the engagement of Washington. The number of new federal grant programs and the aid dollars that went with them more than tripled (from $7 billion in 1960 to $24 billion in 1970), and state and local government financial dependence on funding flowing from Congress increased

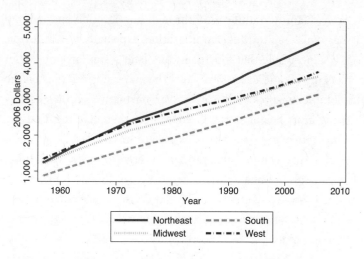

Figure 15. Total state and local tax revenue per capita by region, 1957–2006.

by 35 percent.[27] The War on Poverty exerted considerable control on how the largesse was to be applied, and in this sense the 1960s were the heyday of expanding direct federal spending at the state and local levels.

Richard Nixon was disturbed by this state of affairs, and true to his Republican roots, he set about altering the terms of engagement with the states almost as soon as he entered the White House. Federalism replaced central guidelines as Nixon championed devolution, gradually increasing the use of block grants. Devolution ratcheted up even further under the prodding of Ronald Reagan. He opposed government spending in general and advocated traditional local control while busily collaborating with Office of Management and Budget director David Stockman to "starve the beast."[28] In practice what this meant, according to Conlan, was an end to federal initiatives in domestic policy. The one exception to this rule was the "increasing financial respon-

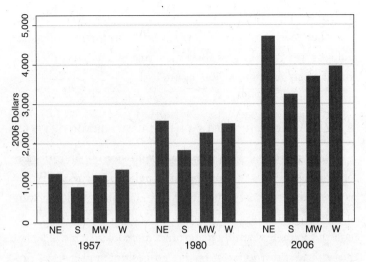

Figure 16. Total state and local tax revenue per capita, averaged across states within regions.

sibilities, including new mandates and expansion of Medicaid eligibility."[29] The retreat of the federal government from direct social spending under Nixon, Reagan, and eventually the Gingrich Congress of the 1990s put increasing pressure on state and local governments to raise revenue both to provide social services and to meet federal matching requirements. It is this that sent state expenditures skyward, requiring ever greater intake to the state coffers, as demonstrated in figure 15, which shows total state and local tax revenue by region in real dollars, that is, after adjusting for inflation. This increased demand set the stage for tax revolts, particularly in the West.

By the early 1990s the love affair with supermajority rules had spread throughout the West. The contagion had the effect of making the West look a great deal like the South in its sources of state and local revenue. Not surprisingly, it also opened a substantial gap in the revenue raised per capita between the regions. In 1957, the first year for which we have data, the distance between the South and the Northeast in per capita state and local tax revenue was about $300 (in 2006 dollars). By 2006, that gap had grown to $1,500 (figure 16).

THE NEW SOUTH MEETS THE OLD SUPERMAJORITIES

Is the reliance on sales tax simply an expression of public distaste for progressive taxation or spending policy in general? Would we see a different tax structure if, for example, the South were to swing toward the Democrats and decide it was time to pour money into their woefully underfunded school systems? The last thirty years provide a test of this proposition and it fails. Several maverick young governors swept the Deep South during that period—Clinton in Arkansas, Riley in Alabama, and Mabus in Mississippi—and they understood all too well that an inadequate system of public education was a barrier to the economic development of the region. Their instincts ran toward progressive solutions, but the political realities they faced put road blocks in front of virtually any effort to raise revenue for the schools, outside of the regressive mechanism of sales tax increases.

Bill Clinton was elected for the first time in Arkansas in 1978 but suffered a defeat in 1982 that taught him a few lessons about the wisdom of coming into conflict with the state's major industries. In particular, he abandoned his initial effort to increase corporate income tax or add a tax on natural gas.[30] In some respects one could argue that he had little choice, given the supermajority requirements in place to prevent increases in these, and most other, types of tax. As Clinton himself pointed out to the *New York Times*, a three-fourths vote of the legislature was required to approve any tax increase other than sales taxes.[31]

Accordingly, in 1983, in response to a state supreme court decision that found the distribution of aid within the kindergarten through twelfth grade education system unconstitutional *(Alma v. Dupree),* Governor Clinton raised the sales tax in Arkansas 33 percent—from 3 to 4 cents per dollar—to fund education. At the time, Arkansas had the most underfinanced school system in the nation, ranking last in per pupil expenditures and teachers' salaries.[32] Clinton's solution received widespread public support.[33] Again in 1991, Clinton asked the state legislature to approve a $200 million education package to be used for teacher salaries, higher education, and preschool and public school programs. These improvements were all to be funded through an increase in sales taxes.[34] When asked whether this wasn't a damaging way to fund improvements in public services, Clinton replied, "Many favor a tax increase but want the money to be raised in a different way. Some say the sales tax is regressive because it falls too heavily on the working class and the poor. Others say the corporate income tax at the upper level will deter economic growth in Arkansas. To the first group I reply that this education program will benefit the children and grandchildren of the working class and the poor more than any other people in the state." Few could object that educational improvement benefits low-income families in the long run, but getting from here to there imposed burdens on poor families in Arkansas that their counterparts outside the region did not face.[35]

The Arkansas experience alerts us to the path dependency involved in the evolution of tax policy in the southern states. Initially the brainchild of conservatives looking to exact revenue from the poorest citizens and the middle class, and to protect the interests of the well heeled, consumption taxes ended up as the favored instrument of liberal Democrats as well. And not because they enjoyed it, or so they said, but because the iron-clad supermajority requirements and tax and spending limits embedded in southern state constitutions left them with few other politically feasible mechanisms for raising revenue.

Does the Arkansas experience represent a general allergy to progressive taxation that is somehow exclusive to the states of the old Confederacy? Not really. In 1972, the Nixon administration's Advisory Commission on Intergovernmental Relations commissioned the Opinion Research Corporation to conduct a national survey of citizens' views of taxation.[36] Nixon was interested in whether Americans would support a national value-added tax as a means of raising federal revenue. The results give us some insight into public understanding of the best and worst forms of taxation. When asked which tax was least fair, 19 percent of the survey respondents nationwide identified the federal income tax; 45 percent, by far the largest group of respondents, pointed to local property taxes. When asked how states should raise revenue if they had to go after "large amounts of new tax dollars," respondents chose a sales tax.[37]

Sales taxes appeal because they are so incremental as to be barely noticeable, while property taxes are paid in lump sums that announce their presence and affect the pocketbook. Moreover, sales taxes are regarded as fair because everyone pays the same rate and households can, arguably, "choose" whether and when to consume and pay the tax, while property and income taxes are progressive and hit high earners harder than those at the bottom. Of course, poor people cannot really choose not to spend money on food, clothing, or transportation to work, which together eat up about 50 percent of their income while rent and utilities consume the rest, and then some. The principle of progressive taxation—which sees the wealthy pay a larger share of the tax bill than the poor—hard fought at the very creation of the federal income tax, has sat uneasily in many parts of the country.

We might conclude from this discussion that supermajority rules and limits on taxation are not particularly important as a barrier to progressive property or income tax, because they are merely codifications of voter sentiment that is more supportive of regressive revenue gathering like sales tax anyway. This may be the case, but sales tax seems to be more palatable throughout the country; the differences in public sentiment, at least in the early 1970s, were not very pronounced. Hence we need another explanation for why the South and increasingly the West are more reliant on sales tax than other parts of the country.[38] The supermajority rules and procedural barriers to increasing virtually any other revenue source may be the reason.

That said, it is reasonable to ask whether the southern penchant for regressive taxation and spending would have been reversed had the supermajority provisions been eliminated. The experience of the HOPE scholarship policy might give us pause on this account because it is not an outgrowth of the distant history but a relatively new instrument for educational investment. In 1993, the state of Georgia was the first to enact a lottery that provided dedicated revenue for college scholarships provided to in-state students. Lotteries are a favorite pastime of low-income and black families in the state, who spend a larger proportion of their income this way than do more affluent or white families. Because HOPE scholarships are awarded to high-achieving high school students—who also tend to be from middle- and upper-income households—the HOPE system represents a regressive transfer of resources from the needy to the well-to-do. Note that the winners are both black and white. Indeed, after the introduction of this scholarship program, black enrollment in Georgia—particularly in the historically black colleges and universities—jumped up by 15 percent while white enrollment rose 3.6 percent.[39]

Clearly race is not the issue here; that said, class may be. "In the year prior to HOPE," C. Cornwell and colleagues tell us, "the state provided $4.9 million of strictly need-based grants and $26 million of total aid. . . . By 2002–3, Georgia's total aid had grown to $397 million annually, while its need-based grants declined to $1.5 million." The shift to merit-based financial aid for college students and away from a means-tested need-based system is putting the squeeze on children from poor households, the group that "contributes" more than any other to lottery earnings.

The HOPE model proved very popular, particularly in the South. What started in Georgia spread to Florida, Kentucky, Louisiana, Mississippi, South Carolina, Tennessee, and West Virginia.[40] To be sure, other states found the program politically appealing, mainly because middle-class beneficiaries are engaged voters. But the epicenter of merit-based financial aid was in the southern states, and this suggests a long cultural tradition of regressive policy, even when the aim is clearly positive: to ease the costs of higher education.

CONCLUSION

In 2009 the stimulus package proposed by President Obama offered states an infusion of resources designed to minimize layoffs of public sector workers and protect the vulnerable by extending unemployment benefits to workers victimized by the gathering storm of recession. One by one, most of the governors in the Deep South (with the exception of Crist in Florida) rejected this helping hand, turning back millions of dollars that would have cushioned the blow of poverty growing in their states. The rest of the nation scratched its head, unable to understand why any governor would refuse resources that would help the residents of a state in economic distress. Some legislatures balked and forced an irritated governor or two to back down, but the political theater was strikingly familiar.

For most of its post-Reconstruction history, not to mention the decades before the Civil War, the South has steadfastly eschewed the social policies that would protect its poor and minority residents, whether children or the elderly in retirement. It has reacted with deep suspicion to federal intrusion, refused funds that would require any form of matching contributions, and then exacerbated the problems of the poor by turning to the most regressive instruments for supporting the public sector. Yet without other effective revenue sources, there are few alternatives.

And why are there few other options? The states' constitutions, amended during the Jim Crow era but harkening all the way back to the pre–Civil War equalization statutes, created almost insurmountable barriers to change. Supermajorities that are extremely difficult to muster and rules that require local tax reforms to pass through the hands of state legislatures and public referendums are just two of the constraints that have helped to ensure that any effort to create a more progressive tax code would face an uphill climb. Hence just as the state of California strangled on its own supermajority requirements in 2010 and nearly found itself bankrupt as a consequence, the state of Alabama remains mired in a tax regime that bears all the hallmarks of the nineteenth century. Large landholders are protected, and ordinary low-wage workers are paying a steeper bill than almost anywhere else in the country.

The family resemblance between Alabama and so much of the rest of the old Confederacy tells us that this is not an accident. The southern states learned from one another how to create and sustain taxation regimes that reinforced racial and class inequality. That legacy is so powerful that when Governor Bob Riley of Alabama, an enlightened Republican, tried to increase taxes to support improvements in the schools in 2003, his initiative was crushed under the weight of the referendum system.[41] "In one fell swoop," the *New York Times* reported, "Mr. Riley is trying to overhaul what many . . . in Montgomery acknowledge is one of the nation's most dysfunctional state governments and drag Alabama's finances, schools and prisons into the 21st century—if not, some might say, the 20th." It was not to be, though, and that was no accident. The pathway to change is almost impossible to negotiate in states with an antitax mentality and powerful barriers to amending tax laws.

CHAPTER THREE

The Geography of Poverty

Alicia Smith lives in a single-wide trailer at the foot of a dirt road so obscure that we could not find it on any map of the region west of Montgomery, Alabama. It took nearly forty minutes to drive from the main highway to Snow Hill, the landmark nearest to Alicia's home. Roads in this part of Alabama are shrouded in thick trees, dripping with Spanish moss. A few houses are visible from the road, but mostly the land is overgrown with vines and shrubs, with the occasional open meadow in the distance. We drove up a long, winding road to the Snow Hill Normal and Industrial Institute hoping to find someone who could tell us where to find Alicia's home, only to find it totally deserted, weeds poking up through the remnants of cement stairs. The commemorative plaque outside recalled that the school shut down in 1972, when desegregation opened opportunities for black students to enroll in white institutions.

After flagging down a passing car, we were directed back to the main highway and told to keep our eyes open for a roadside tavern, which turned out to be more of a shack. Opposite

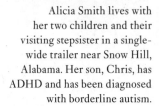

Alicia Smith lives with her two children and their visiting stepsister in a single-wide trailer near Snow Hill, Alabama. Her son, Chris, has ADHD and has been diagnosed with borderline autism.

the tavern, we found a winding dirt road that opened out onto a scraggly meadow with trailers dotted here and there and a horse tethered out behind one of them. Alicia's trailer was just opposite the horse.

The land underneath her home belongs to a hard-pressed white family that rents out several old and poorly maintained trailers in the hollow for the price of the land taxes—about $100 a month. It is the maximum that Alicia can afford. It isn't worth much more than that: the kitchen floor is rotting, the carpets are worn and stained; the bunk bed her two children—eight-year-old Chris and his two-year-old sister—share when their teenage stepsister is not around nearly scrapes the ceiling of the bedroom. They have lived in this trailer ever since it became clear that they were no longer welcome to share the home of a friend in McWilliams, twenty miles from Snow Hill, where they had been doubled up for some time.

We pulled our car onto the grass outside the Smith home just in time to see the family unload a month's worth of groceries from the trunk of a friend's car. The Smiths have no wheels and depend on the kindness of this woman (from their church)—and a $20 fee—to travel into the nearest city to shop for food. The

Alicia's trailer sits on scrubland off a dirt road. Without a car it is impossible to go anywhere from her home.

An entire month's shopping on the floor of Alicia's kitchen. She can afford to go to the store only once every four weeks because she must pay a church friend $20 to take her there and back.

trip takes forty minutes each way, and so the whole family makes a day of it, leaving at 7 A.M. and returning with an enormous pile of groceries and a Greenville, Alabama, Wal-Mart receipt that is nearly three feet long. Alicia purchased a box of clementines, some bananas, a precious strip steak, tomatoes, shredded carrots, and some chicken, the sum total of fresh food her family will have for the next month. The rest of the list was selected to last with minimal refrigeration. Potato chips, crackers, sausage, six loaves of white bread, Cheetos and Fritos, grape jelly, vienna sausage, hot dogs, meat sticks, dill pickles, spaghetti sauce, canned soup, and snack cakes were piled up on the floor in dozens of plastic bags. Alicia is a heavy woman whose daily diet, drawn from these mega shopping trips, undoubtedly exacerbates her medical problems, including a bad back.

Chris, the eight-year-old, has been diagnosed with borderline autism and ADHD and, we were told, can barely read. His teachers recommended that he be held back in school; hence he is just completing first grade for the second time. He is on a steady dosage of a drug (whose name we didn't catch) designed to increase his concentration. Alicia complains that without his other medications she would not be able to get Chris to sleep at night. His adorable little sister shows no signs of behavior problems and is an intensely curious child. But she is asthmatic, as is her mother, and depends on the use of inhalers, especially during the high-pollen season.

No one likes to be dependent, least of all Alicia, who has a feisty personality and is given to boredom if she has nothing to keep her occupied. All in all, she would rather work, and she has made good on that commitment for most of her adult life. She worked for nine years as a certified nursing assistant and then put in another three in telemarketing. For a time after she left Cin-

Alicia suffers from back and knee problems because of her weight and old back injuries from her work as a nursing assistant. From her chair she can see the computer screen that connects her to an online course in early childhood education.

gular's telemarketing division, Alicia had a job at Dollar General, a cheap clothing and household goods chain that can be found in most of the towns in southern Alabama. For a working poor family, though, staying on the job ends up costing too much.

"I made $6.50 an hour," Alicia told us. "Three-fourths of my check was going to someone else for gas, for transportation to work. The more I worked, the more I had to pay out. Cost me $20 a day to get to work. We can't afford a car. I was having to depend on [other people]. Then it got to where sometimes I could catch rides and someone else could bring me home. That would save $10 here and there."

By the time she was done paying to get to her job, there was virtually nothing left of her wages. But there was no housing the family could afford any closer to Dollar General. This trap is a tough one for poor people in rural regions of the country. While the urban poor can catch buses or ride the subways, their counterparts in Snow Hill or Pine Apple, Alabama, are in serious trouble if they cannot afford a car. When the price of gas climbs—and it is always higher in remote places anyway—the rural poor hemorrhage money and end up dropping out of the labor market. Wages are too low to make work pay under these circumstances. And in the states where they live, the benefits for Temporary Assistance for Needy Families (TANF) are set at such meager levels that without federal contributions through food stamps, they would sink into the dust.

For now, the family relies on the funds it receives from Supplemental Security Income for Chris because of his learning disabilities and autism—$674 a month—and $215 in a TANF stipend for the little girl. The federal government kicks in for the food stamps. The Women, Infants, and Children Program (WIC), which covers only particular foods (like milk, eggs, bread, and peanut butter), adds to the food budget. Alicia is quick to point out that without food stamps, the family would starve. They can barely pay their bills anyway. "We don't get beat up with the rent," she admits, "but the utilities!

"The electric bill was just under $200 this month. But we're just getting around to the part of the year when we have to use the air conditioner. Our bill next month is going to be $220. If it goes over $250, we're in trouble. We have to pay a $90 per month phone bill. . . . The water bill . . . well, we went from having a bill under $40. Now it's $70. Last month it was $100. . . . I don't know what's going on with that. Plus we pay $60 for cable, but it's worth it because there are channels for all of us. We budget $150–$160 a month for household stuff like toilet paper, toothpaste, mouthwash, deodorant, razors. Diapers. It would be a blessing if we could get [the youngest] potty trained, because we're ready to spend that $35 on something else!"

Perhaps in another few months.

That $90 phone bill is a big expense for such a poor household. It has zoomed up ever since Alicia started relying on her telephone to link her (through a dial-up service) to the Internet and her favorite online college course in early childhood education. Like Beatrice Coleman in Birmingham (see the Preface), Alicia is heavily indebted for the privilege. So far, she owes $10,000 and has another year to go to finish the course. Alicia hopes it will help her learn to deal with Chris's autism and ADHD problems, but the online community is also important to her because she is so isolated in her little trailer. Her social world is confined to her children and the family in the trailer next door. She can go for many days, even weeks, without seeing anyone else. Being part of an online class gives Alicia other people to interact with—if not in person, at least in a virtual world.

It is hard to be poor in places like Snow Hill. At the end of the month, she is stone-broke, standing by the mailbox waiting for public benefit checks to arrive. They don't amount to much, but they are all the family has. Like Bea, Alicia faces a lifetime on this treadmill. Where she was once a steady worker, she now lives on such a thin margin that she cannot afford to take the only jobs going in the retail shops at minimum wage. And these days, there is little else available.

Nobody is running new shifts in the factories that once provided jobs to the working poor in this region of the country. The women we met in Pine Apple, Alabama, one of the closest towns to Snow Hill, used to work in a textile factory that produced underwear but were laid off the previous month; the lumber companies fired the men six months earlier because the construction industry is at a standstill. For many years, the South outstripped other parts of the country in job growth. Northeastern and midwestern firms were streaming to the southern states, attracted by low business taxes, the weakness of unions, and the low wages of the region. Northern workers with southern roots followed the jobs.[1] Tony Boddie, an African American man in his forties we talked to in a daytime church shelter that provides free meals to the needy in Birmingham, had come down South with his wife, Senora, and kids decades earlier when the steel mills and auto plants of his native Buffalo, New York, shut down. All of the men in Tony's family—his dad, his brothers, and Tony himself—were laid off within weeks of one another. Not one to wait around for his own funeral, Tony picked up his family and moved to Atlanta, where he found work in fiber optics with Verizon. That ended in a wave of offshoring. The only place left to go, besides the homeless shelter where Tony and Senora were living when we met them, was the land his uncle bought years before near Birmingham. They were only welcome for a time.

· · ·

The wide gap that separates Americans in the South from their cousins in other parts of the country is neither a consequence of the concentration of African Americans in the region nor an outgrowth of the higher levels of poverty found there. Among blacks, whites, and the poor, southerners look significantly worse on most measures of well-being than their counterparts in, for example, Michigan—a state burdened by industrial decline—or Illinois, with its large urban ghettos. What's more, there is evidence to suggest that southerners (particularly of African American descent) have more problematic health outcomes even when they move out of the region and live for years in the Northeast, for example.[2]

In this chapter, we explore the ways in which the southern states diverge from the rest of the country with respect to poverty and related outcomes.[3] This sets the stage for the central inquiry of this book, namely, the role of taxation in creating and sustaining the disparities, the issue to which we turn in chapter 4.

HOUSEHOLD INCOME

It is most appropriate to begin by looking at household income. As map 1 makes clear, in 2008—the most recent year for which we have data—nearly every southern state was below the median on household income. Indeed eight of the ten lowest-ranked states on this measure are below the Mason-Dixon Line.

Median income tells us little about the proportion of the population that experiences poverty, since residents could, in theory, be tightly packed around this central mark. With the exception of Virginia and Florida, no southern state had less than 13 percent of the population below the federal poverty line in 2008 (map 2). Most of them look a good deal worse. Louisiana, Arkansas, Kentucky, Texas, Georgia, and Mississippi all weigh in with more than 15 percent below the poverty line.[4]

Perhaps even more striking is the proportion of these state populations that suffer from *extreme* poverty, meaning below 50 percent of the federal poverty line. This is the unfortunate fate of nearly 9 percent of the people in Mississippi, with many other southern states close on its heels. The western states, especially those with large Hispanic populations, are seeing the ranks of the poor grow, as well. By contrast, few northern or eastern

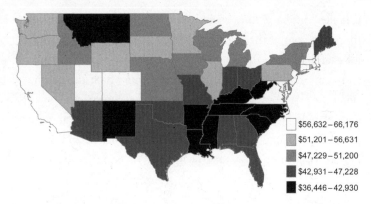

Map 1. Median household income, 2008. Source: Current Population Survey, U.S. Census Bureau and Bureau of Labor Statistics.

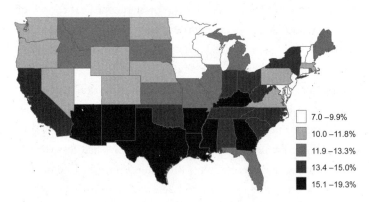

Map 2. Population in poverty, 2008. Percentage of individuals below the federal poverty line. Source: Current Population Survey, U.S. Census Bureau and Bureau of Labor Statistics.

states have poverty rates that exceeded the national median of 13 percent, and the proportion of their populations that suffer from extreme poverty is generally below 5 percent.

The distribution of children in poverty parallels that of the general population. The states with the highest child poverty

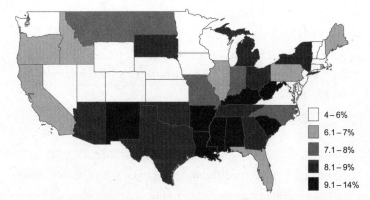

Map 3. Children in extreme poverty, 2008. Percentage of children living below 50 percent of the federal poverty line. Source: American Community Survey, U.S. Census Bureau.

rates (15–21 percent of children under 18) stands out as a solid mass of southern states, with only slightly more favorable numbers for the southeastern seaboard states that have benefitted from economic growth in recent years. The large northeastern states of New York, Ohio, and Michigan also have high child poverty rates, as do some southwestern states (e.g., New Mexico and Arizona, with their large immigrant populations), but the most serious concentration of poor children remains in the Deep South.

Even more worrisome is the high proportion of children who live in extreme poverty (less than 50 percent of the federal poverty line; see map 3). In the Midwest and some of the largest northeastern states, 7–9 percent of the children suffer from this hardship, but the South stands out for its much higher concentration of children whose households live in extreme poverty. We know that experiencing poverty in childhood has devastating consequences that last a lifetime, even for those who clear the poverty line in adulthood.[5] Individuals who have experienced poverty in childhood are less likely to graduate from high school and are more likely to have out-of-wedlock births; both of these outcomes set young people on the road to a lifetime below the poverty line.[6]

MATERIAL HARDSHIP

Critics might object that the federal poverty line, which is not adjusted for differences in cost of living, is a misleading standard for assessing regional differences. If it costs a lot less to live in Mississippi than it does in Minnesota, the use of a national standard will overstate the deprivation families are exposed to in the southern region. This is a fair point and to contend with it, we must turn to other kinds of data.

The federal government maintains a large data base—the Survey of Income and Program Participation (SIPP)—that asks a battery of questions designed to assess the hardships households experience: How often do people forgo visits to the doctor? Find themselves unable to pay the utility bills? Become exposed to vermin? Lack basic household necessities such as a phone? These are the realities of living with poverty.

We examined the data from the SIPP's Adult Well-Being topical module, administered as part of the fifth wave of the 2004 panel. As table 4 suggests, there are some regional differences.

Controlling for household income, a variety of poverty-related conditions are more prevalent in the South than in the rest of the country. This includes living in a home infested by vermin or other pests (14 percent higher in the South), not having a home phone or a cell phone (59 percent higher), and living in a household whose phone was disconnected in the past year because of

Table 4

Logistic regression: Material hardship in the South
controlling for (log) household income

Measures of material hardship	Odds ratio for South
Home infestation (mice, roaches, etc.)	1.14***
No home phone or cell phone	1.59***
Telephone disconnected in past year due to lack of payment	1.20***
Did not see doctor when needed	1.29***
Did not see dentist when needed	1.14***

SOURCE: Author's calculation using data from 2004 Survey of Income and Program Participation, Adult Well-Being Topical Module, http://www.census.gov/sipp/.

NOTES: $N = 37,294$; household weights used; ***$p < .01$; **$p < .05$; *$p < .1$.

lack of payment (20 percent higher). Access to medical care is more problematic in the South. The odds that someone in the household did not see a doctor or go to the hospital when needed at some point in the last year are 29 percent higher in the South. Similarly, the inability to see a dentist was 14 percent higher. The difference between the South and the rest of the country on each of these measures is statistically significant (at the $p < .01$ level).[7]

We conclude from our analysis that the lower cost of living in the South, compared to other regions of the country, does not undermine our reliance on the federal poverty line as a benchmark. As far as material hardship is concerned, it is worse to be poor in the South than in the rest of the country. The conditions we associate with poverty are more prevalent *among* southerners who are below the federal poverty line than they are in other parts of the country.

HEALTH DISPARITIES

Income matters for many reasons, most especially for the ways in which it translates into the kinds of hardships discussed in the previous section. But there are two other "bottom lines" that we associate with poverty that are indirectly affected by income: health and education. As we have seen in the cases of Beatrice Coleman and Alicia Smith, both of whom are jobless because they are disabled, poor health creates a cascade of unfortunate consequences, including reducing their earning power. Both women are poorly educated—though trying to catch up online—and that limits their options in the labor market, often to precisely those kinds of backbreaking jobs that have actually damaged their backs. Because of this connection between health and poverty, it is important to examine the regional distribution of health indicators.

If we were to rely on one simple measure above all others to assess the health of a community, we would probably pick life expectancy. On this score, the news for the southern states is particularly sobering. The ten worst states for average life expectancy are all southern states—every last one. The southwestern states with large, poor Latino populations are, interestingly, in the middle of the pack. As map 4 makes clear, the South has the dubious distinction (along with the District of Columbia) of the lowest life expectancy in the country. Not a single northern, western, or midwestern state is to be found in this category.

When we examine the components that contribute to life expectancy, we get a finer-grained picture of the southern health disadvantage. We begin with the end: mortality. Here we follow the standard demographer's practice of adjusting the data for the age distribution of each state in order to clarify how death rates

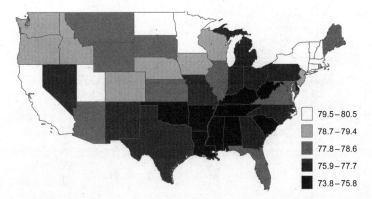

Map 4. Life expectancy, 2005. Source: U.S. Human Development Project and CDC.

vary apart from the age profile (map 5). The South is noticeable for its high level of mortality per 100,000.

Infant mortality is a particularly sensitive barometer of health, and understanding its contours is important because measures of life expectancy are so heavily affected by it. Countries like India have low life expectancy less because their middle-aged people die young than because millions of babies die in infancy and lower the overall life expectancy of the country. As a developed nation, we tend to think infant mortality is no longer a serious issue, and relative to much poorer countries, this is certainly the case. The U.S. average is approximately 6.9 deaths per 1,000 live births (while India comes in at 68, and Mexico and China at 25 and 27, respectively).[8] Nonetheless, there are some significant regional differences in infant mortality. As map 6 shows, high rates of infant mortality are particularly common in the Old South, as well as among the northern states that contain large urban ghettos (such as Washington, DC; Detroit; and Baltimore).

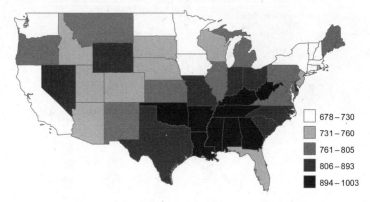

Map 5. Age-adjusted mortality, 2005 (deaths per 100,000). Source: CDC National Center for Health Statistics.

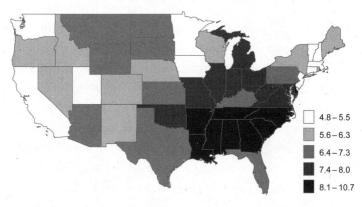

Map 6. Infant mortality, 2003–2005 (deaths per 1,000 live births). Source: CDC Division of Vital Statistics.

Infant mortality occurs for many reasons, but perhaps the most prevalent factor is the incidence of premature births, in which babies are more likely to be of low weight. Map 7 shows a significant cluster of preterm births in the southern states.

Among mothers in the southern states, we find high propor-

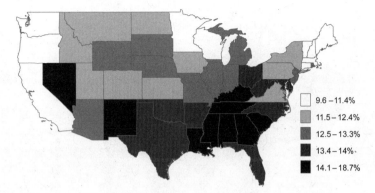

Map 7. Preterm births as a percentage of all births, 2006. Source: CDC National Center for Health Statistics.

tions of premature births and, not surprising, low-birth-weight babies as well. Babies who are born at a low weight are at risk for all kinds of health and developmental problems throughout the life course. Adults who were low-birth-weight babies seem to be at increased risk for high blood pressure, type 2 (adult onset) diabetes, and heart disease.[9] Hence the concentrated incidence of babies with these problems creates extraordinary burdens for their families and high health care costs that can emerge at the onset and continue into later life. The southern states are in poor shape at both ends of the life span.

The mothers of low-birth-weight children are often teenagers who receive less medical attention and may be less attentive to dietary practices that matter for a developing fetus. Concern over teenage childbearing has been with us for many years,[10] but it is almost always conceptualized as a national problem. One look at the regional distribution of teen birth rates per 1,000 (map 8) makes it clear that this is a major problem specifically for the southern and southwestern states.[11]

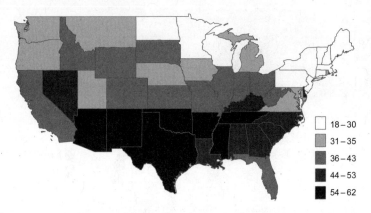

Map 8. Teen birth rate, 2005 (per 1,000). Source: Guttmacher Institute.

As a nation, we struggle with obesity, never more so than now. Medical professionals and public health researchers fill the airwaves with warnings about the relationship between adult weight and a host of chronic and deadly diseases that catch up with us in the elder years. But the problem of obesity does not begin in adulthood. Instead, it starts (and has been getting worse) among the nation's children. Map 9 makes it clear that this is indeed a nationwide epidemic. No state escapes unscathed, but some are worse than others, and once again, as a region, the South looks particularly bad. In the majority of southern states, more than one-third of children ten to seventeen years of age are classified as obese or overweight.[12] The pounds do not melt away as they age, either. Instead, we see a national problem of overweight adults spread far and wide, with a cluster of extremely troubled states (Tennessee, Alabama, and Mississippi) where over 30 percent of the adult population is officially obese and fully two-thirds are overweight (map 10).

This pattern of obesity coincides with the infamous "stroke belt" that wraps its tentacles around the southern states. For

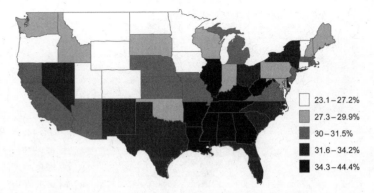

Map 9. Percentage of children ten to seventeen who are overweight or obese, 2007. Source: Data Resource Center for Child and Adolescent Health.

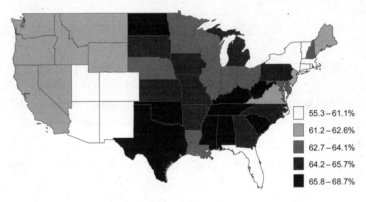

Map 10. Percentage of adults who are overweight or obese, 2007. Source: CDC National Center for Health Statistics.

every 100,000 people, approximately 800 die in any given year. Map 11 displays the number of those deaths attributable to stroke and related conditions. The southern states stand out because the incidence of stroke-related death is so much higher than it is in other regions, including the high-immigration states of Arizona, New Mexico, and California, whose citizens are far less

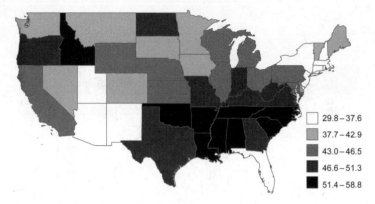

Map 11. Deaths from stroke and other cerebrovascular diseases, 2006 (per 100,000). Source: CDC National Center for Health Statistics.

likely to die of these obesity-linked conditions.[13] Being overweight, combined with low levels of physical activity, a pattern strikingly evident in the Deep South,[14] is a killer combination.

Health differences of this magnitude impose on the southern states in a variety of ways, first and foremost on the well-being of families that must contend with debilitating disease and early death, as well as on health care systems that strain to care for the disabled. The public purse is burdened by extraordinary costs for problems appearing early on in the life course,[15] hence lasting for decades before the final toll is taken. While access to medical care is a huge benefit once disease emerges, it does not tell us very much about inequalities in the onset of illness.[16] Socioeconomic status is a more powerful predictor of health outcomes, and poor health boomerangs back on individuals to lower their prospects for greater income and more rewarding employment.

IS IT RACE?

It might be objected that because minorities are more susceptible to all of the health conditions discussed here (from low birth weight and teen births to obesity and the diseases that stem from it), these observations of regional disparities in health are merely picking up on the distribution of minority populations that remain largely concentrated in the southern states.

Yet when we look at the health outcomes for whites, we see that the pattern holds for all of the problems we have discussed thus far.[17] For example, the rate of infant mortality for white babies is exceptionally high in the southern region. Seven of the worst ten states for infant mortality within this race group are found in the South (map 12).

The comparatively high rates of white infant mortality are probably linked to the incidence of low-birth-weight babies, which is more pronounced among southern whites than it is among their counterparts in other regions (map 13). Indeed, every southern state (except Virginia) is above national average for percentage of all white births that are low-weight births.

Shifting away from the afflictions of early childhood to the other end of the life span, we see that whites in the South are more likely to die from heart disease than their counterparts elsewhere. Six of the worst eight states for cardiovascular-related death rates among whites are in the South (map 14).

Map 15 examines the same kind of data for whites who die from stroke or cerebrovascular disease. Once again, the South stands out for the poor outcomes for its white population.

While racial minorities are disproportionately poor and hence suffer from conditions associated with poverty—including these

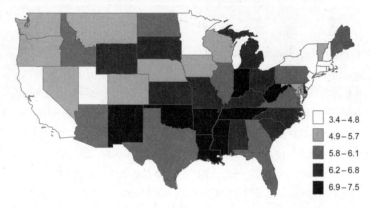

Map 12. Infant mortality rate for non-Hispanic whites, 2003–2005 (per 1,000 live births). Source: CDC Division of Vital Statistics.

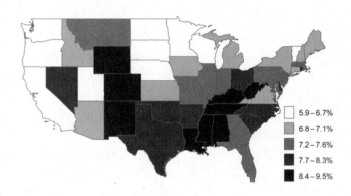

Map 13. Births of low birth weight as a percentage of all births in non-Hispanic whites, 2006. Source: CDC National Center for Health Statistics.

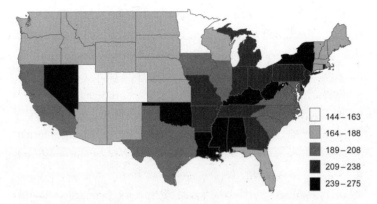

Map 14. Deaths from heart disease in non-Hispanic whites, 2006 (per 100,000).
Source: CDC National Center for Health Statistics.

	144 – 163
	164 – 188
	189 – 208
	209 – 238
	239 – 275

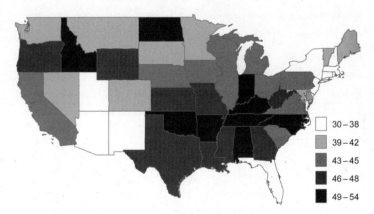

Map 15. Deaths from stroke and other cerebrovascular diseases in non-Hispanic
whites, 2006 (per 100,000). Source: CDC National Center for Health Statistics.

	30 – 38
	39 – 42
	43 – 45
	46 – 48
	49 – 54

pernicious health outcomes—to a greater degree than whites do, the data discussed here make it clear that the health outcomes that plague the South are not confined to the black population. To be sure, blacks in the South look worse than their northern and midwestern counterparts on a host of health indicators.[18] Living in the South produces poor health outcomes for whites as well.[19]

Is this a reflection of inequality in general? That is, is the internal economic inequality in southern states, which is very pronounced indeed, the reason why we see such poor health outcomes? Some scholars maintain this is the case.[20] Princeton economist Angus Deaton objects. He argues that the presence of a large black population is driving the bad outcomes for all concerned and that the findings on inequality wash out when we control for the percentage of the population that is African American.[21] Yet others claim to have found an error in Deaton's work that, when corrected, restores the impact of inequality on health net of the racial composition.[22] The matter is clearly still controversial; in the chapter that follows, we add taxes to the discussion and argue that they play a role in driving these results.

EDUCATIONAL ATTAINMENT

In the years following World War II, a high-growth industrial economy provided millions of jobs for modestly skilled Americans who poured into the factories and the construction companies that produced the refrigerators, cars, and houses that defined the country's enviable standard of living. A man could take a unionized blue collar job and hope to support a family on his own steam, clearing the way for his wife to take care of the legions of baby boom children. Life was always harder for minority families, whose women had to work when their white counterparts had the option to stay home. But even for African Americans, the international dominance of the American economy meant increased opportunity and a higher standard of living than their parents had to accept in the prewar period.

As countless studies have explained, this portrait no longer holds. Manufacturing has departed the Rust Belt cities, only to reappear in nonunionized parts of the country (especially the South and the Southwest) and, increasingly, offshore altogether. The rewards of education have grown spectacularly as we have transitioned to a postindustrial society. Even the factories expect the workforce of today to be at ease with personal computers and able to master tasks that require fairly sophisticated reading and math skills.[23] Skill-biased technological change, the term economists use to describe what happened to the demands in the labor market for educated workers and the concomitant demise of the low-skilled job market, has widened the wage gap between well and poorly educated Americans.[24]

Regions with low levels of human capital feel the consequences of these trends. While they benefit from the arrival of industries looking for inexpensive labor, the advantage may be short-lived. Even the lowest-paid American workers earn vastly more than their counterparts in India or China. The low road will not help a region compete for industries that depend on highly skilled workers. Disparities in educational attainment matter: they are implicated more generally in the economic health of the regions.

High levels of high school dropouts (map 16) are particularly toxic indicators of a region in trouble. Low educational attainment often leads to a lifetime spent below the poverty line. It is therefore a worry that southern teenagers leave school at far

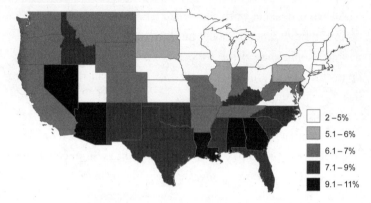

	2 – 5%
	5.1 – 6%
	6.1 – 7%
	7.1 – 9%
	9.1 – 11%

Map 16. Percentage of teens sixteen to nineteen who are high school drop-outs, 2007. Source: American Community Survey, U.S. Census Bureau.

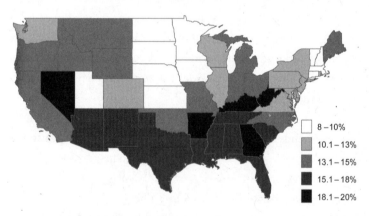

	8 – 10%
	10.1 – 13%
	13.1 – 15%
	15.1 – 18%
	18.1 – 20%

Map 17. Percentage of persons eighteen to twenty-four not attending school, not working, and with no degree beyond high school, 2008. Source: American Community Survey, U.S. Census Bureau.

higher rates than their counterparts everywhere else in the nation. The picture for young adults is not much more encouraging. Among the nation's twenty-five-year-olds, the proportion with at least a high school diploma is lower in the South than any other region. Indeed, the ten worst-performing states on this score are—with the exception of California—all in the Deep South.[25]

Perhaps even more striking are the rates of "idleness," a catch-all concept to cover those who are not in school or the military and not employed. A dark swath cuts across the whole of the South and the Southwest (map 17). A substantial proportion of the region's young adults are disconnected from the worlds of work, schooling, or military service.

What, then, are they doing? The answers are no doubt myriad, but one striking finding comes from the data on incarceration. Sociologist Bruce Western has investigated the astounding rise in imprisonment in the United States, a trend that has paralleled the increasing inequality in society in general. Over the last thirty years, the prison population has soared to over two million people, a sevenfold increase over previous decades. Black men who drop out of high school are especially likely to see the inside of the jailhouse. Sixty percent of those in their early thirties have been in prison.[26] Among the fifteen states with the highest rates of incarceration per capita, ten are in the South (map 18).

Why? The answer lies partly in crime rates. The South is entirely above the median in murder rates, and eight of the fifteen worst states on this score are to be found in the region (map 19).[27] Property crime—burglary in particular—displays a similar regional distribution.[28] But crime rates alone do not

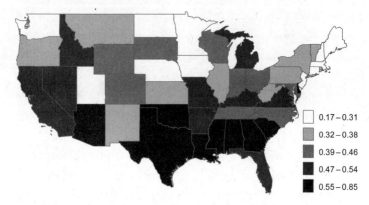

Map 18. Prison population per capita, 2007. Source: Prison Population from U.S. Department of Justice, Bureau of Justice Statistics.

drive incarceration; how states react to crime plays a significant role. On this score, the South emerges as particularly punitive and, accordingly, sustains a very large prison population per capita.[29]

Poor education leaves young people (and the adults they become) with fewer opportunities in the labor market. As economist Richard Freeman has shown, deterioration in job prospects boosts the crime rate,[30] and the supply of young men, particularly young black men, who are failing in school and falling into crime has risen as inequality has grown. At the same time, we have criminalized minor drug offenses in ways that send an increasing proportion of these offenders to prison. Southern states have taken that path to a greater degree than other regions of the country.[31] A negative cycle of poor educational attainment, mixed with a toxic level of unemployment and a punitive approach to criminal behavior, results in high incarceration rates, which further depress the labor market potential of a huge part of the southern population.

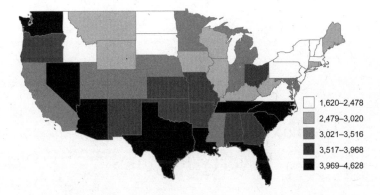

Map 19. Property crime, 2006 (per 100,000). Source: U.S. Department of Justice, Bureau of Justice Statistics.

1,620–2,478
2,479–3,020
3,021–3,516
3,517–3,968
3,969–4,628

CONCLUSION

The regional disparities that separate the South from the rest of the country are pronounced. Whether we look at household income, health outcomes, educational attainment, labor force participation, or crime, the patterns remain constant: the South looks worse on all of these measures. We cannot chalk the difference up to the geography of race. Although the history of racial division in the South is certainly implicated in the depth of poverty experienced by its African American population, the poverty-related patterns discussed in this chapter are hardly confined to blacks. Whites in the South look bad on most of these outcomes, as well, relative to their counterparts in the rest of the country.

We must look beyond race, then, to understand how the structural conditions created by social policies that evolved over time in the South laid the groundwork for the inequalities that separate the citizens of the region from their counterparts in the rest of the country.

CHAPTER FOUR

Tax Traps and Regional Poverty Regimes

The regional concentration of poverty poses serious problems for the whole country. But it remains for us to show that state tax codes bear any responsibility for the situation. Are high taxes on the poor related to social problems like excess mortality, out-of-wedlock childbearing, crime, and low educational attainment? In this chapter we answer in the affirmative: controlling for a host of competing possibilities (the racial composition of each state, patterns of state spending, proportions of the state population below the poverty line, and so forth), tax liabilities assessed on poor households are related to state-level mortality, high school completion, the proportion of births to unmarried mothers, and rates of property and violent crime.

Our analysis employs state and year fixed-effects regression models that look within each state and ask, over time, whether changes in the tax liabilities of poor households affect outcomes such as mortality and crime. The virtue of the fixed-effects approach is that it enables us to net out anything unique to a particular state that could explain why its taxation level is high or low, as well as anything external to it that changes over time and affects all states equally (for example, a change in federal policy).

To the extent that we can show a robust relationship between regressive taxation and negative outcomes in our fixed-effects models *within* states, we will argue that the same mechanism accounts for the significant differences *between* states in poverty-related outcomes. We already know that tax policies create significant differences in the money that poor households have at the end of the day. A family of three at the poverty line in Massachusetts can depend on an annual income of nearly $2,300 more than the same family in Mississippi because the Northeast favors refundable credits while the southern states are more likely to take money out of the pockets of these poor families. Here we demonstrate that differences in taxes paid by poor families are associated with a variety of social ills at the state level. We turn to other research to extend our findings to the individual level as well.

WHAT DO THE POOR PAY IN TAX?

Estimating the tax burden on the poor is a complicated endeavor. In a 2005 report, economists Hassett and Moore attempted to estimate the tax burden on several hypothetical family types to demonstrate that, in the aggregate, the tax burden on the poor has decreased in recent decades, mainly because of increases in the federal Earned Income Tax Credit (EITC), as shown in chapter 5. Although their interest was primarily in national trends, Hassett and Moore made a concerted effort to estimate state and local tax liability to calculate accurately the full tax burden on the poor. We rely on their original work but focus attention on how a poor family—we'll call them the Joneses—fares in different states.[1]

We began by asking what kind of tax liabilities households at the poverty line face in each state. Income tax presents relatively few problems; we know how each state assesses the income of its tax-filing families. The National Bureau of Economic Research maintains a TAXSIM database and a microsimulation model that makes use of both household tax data and administrative information on tax rules by state.[2] Using TAXSIM, we determined the tax rates that applied to a hypothetical family of three—one adult and two dependent children—whose income was exactly at the federal poverty line for every year for which we have data on the outcomes we care about (roughly 1982–2008). We note that changing the structure of the hypothetical family used in the tax simulations does not affect the substantive conclusions about variations across states. The estimated total state and local tax burden on a family of three with one working adult and a family of four with two working adults is correlated at 0.95.

It is important to factor in the credits that different states provide as well, so the total state income tax burden for the Jones family consists of the state income tax rate offset by whatever credits each state provides, refundable or not. Thus we have included in our calculations any state earned income tax credits, renter's credits, child care credits, and sales and excise tax rebates (e.g., rebates on the sales tax on food in Idaho).[3] Map 20 displays the range of state income tax liabilities for a family of three at the federal poverty line.

The southern states all rest above the zero tax liability line—as do a number of non-southern states. This means they collect income taxes from single-parent households earning at or below the federal poverty line. There are no southern states below the zero tax liability line. Several non-southern states provide credits such that their poor families not only do not pay any state

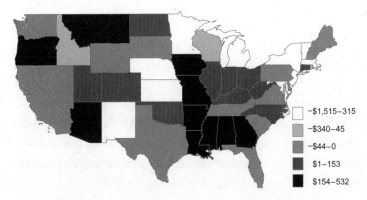

Map 20. State income tax liability for a family of three at the poverty line, 2008. Source: Authors' calculations.

tax but actually end up ahead of the game: they receive a check because the state provides a refundable credit.

Estimating the impact of consumption taxes (e.g., sales taxes) is more complicated. How much do poor families like the Joneses have to pay in sales tax on food, medicine, clothing, and other goods? While the expenses that families actually incur differ to some degree from state to state (winter coats in New York, shorts in Florida), the estimates for what our hypothetical family of three would pay on a basic basket of goods were derived by summing, across all of the states, the information contained in the Consumer Expenditure Survey, which is conducted every year by the U.S. Census Bureau. The Consumer Expenditure Survey provides information on the ways in which Americans spend their money by family type and income levels. Consumption data were pooled for three-person families with incomes just above and just below the federal poverty line for every year between 1982 and 2008, to arrive at a national estimate of what families like the Joneses spend.[4]

Once we know what poor families spend, we need to figure

out how much tax they have to pay at the state and local levels. Different states, and many localities, tax the same goods differently. Some states tax food while others exempt it; some exempt food at the state level but impose a sales tax on food at the local level. The variations are many. To determine how much our hypothetical family would pay in sales tax, the uniform "consumption basket"—the goods our family purchases in a year—is multiplied by the sales tax rate they would face in each state, for every kind of purchase, for every year.[5]

We are particularly interested in taxes on food (for home consumption, not restaurant meals) because of their impact on diet and, downstream, on health outcomes. Fresh fruit and vegetables are expensive, high-quality protein is costly, and carbohydrates and fatty foods are relatively cheap, as well as filling. When food taxes are levied on top of the basic cost of food, we can expect to see poor families substituting lower-cost food for the more healthful but pricier market basket. This may be one of the routes by which the tax burden on the poor ends up affecting mortality.

As of 2008, thirty-one states and the District of Columbia fully exempted food for home consumption from state and local sales tax. The remaining nineteen states treated food differently:

- Two states—Alabama and Mississippi—treated food like any other good and taxed groceries at the full state and local rate.

- Five states—Louisiana, Georgia, South Carolina, North Carolina, and Alaska—exempted food from the state sales tax but allowed localities to tax food.

- Seven states—Arkansas, Illinois, Missouri, Tennessee, Utah, Virginia, and West Virginia—taxed food but at a lower rate than the overall state sales tax rate.

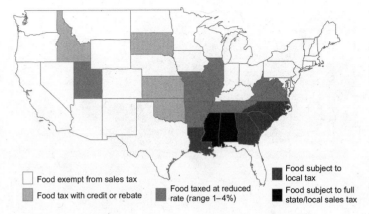

Map 21. Tax treatment of food for home consumption, 2008. Source: Federation of Tax Administrators.

• Five states—Hawaii, Idaho, Kansas, Oklahoma, and South Dakota—taxed food but offered a rebate or tax credit to offset cost to low-income consumers.

As map 21 shows, there is a notable southern pattern in the taxation of food for home consumption. Alabama stands out as exceptionally regressive if we consider that the state not only fully taxes food but does so at a combined state and local tax rate of up to 12 percent, the highest in the nation.

The sales tax figures represented in map 22 capture the estimated combined taxes paid on all the clothing, food, and tangible goods in our consumption basket that were compiled using state tax policy handbooks from 1982 to 2008.[6] The variation between the states in the taxes they exact from poor families for exactly the same annual expenditures are considerable, but six of the ten most regressive states are in the South, and a seventh, Kansas, is a border state.

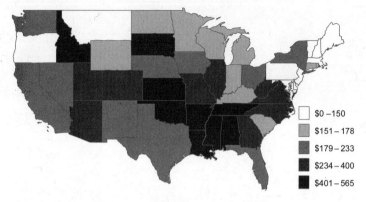

Map 22. State and local sales tax liability for a family of three at the federal poverty line, 2008. Source: Authors' calculations.

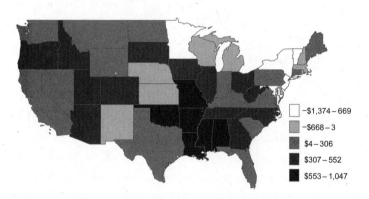

Map 23. Total state and local tax liability for a family of three at the federal poverty line, 2008. Source: Authors' calculations.

Summing all forms of taxation, we see in map 23 that the total liabilities faced by southern families at the poverty line are higher compared to what families in other parts of the country have to pay.

TAX LIABILITIES AND STATE OUTCOMES
ON POVERTY-RELATED CONDITIONS

Now that we know what the Jones household has to pay in taxes, it remains for us to determine the relationship between the liability for poor families and the outcomes we care about most.[7] Over the past twenty-five years, there has been a dramatic divergence in how states tax the poor. Since the early 1980s many southern and western states have *increased* taxes on the poor while most northeastern states have significantly *reduced* the tax burden on those under the poverty line, trends we explore in the next chapter. By 2008 most poor families in the Northeast actually had a *negative* state and local tax liability; that is, they actually received a rebate in the form of a state EITC or other refundable credit. Such a divergence over time and across states enables us to investigate how increasing or decreasing the tax burden on the poor affects the poverty-related outcomes documented in the previous chapter. To do so, we turn to state fixed-effects models, which provide two primary advantages over cross-sectional analyses. First, by fixing the intercept of each state, we are able to net out all state-specific characteristics that do not change over time. Second, by including "year effects" in the model, we are able to net out changes that affect all states equally, such as a shift in federal policy.

What we are essentially modeling, then, is change. Holding constant the baseline differences in poverty-related outcomes and state characteristics that do not change over time, how does an increase in taxes on the poor relate to the outcomes that interest us? By concentrating on change, fixed-effects models allow us to better isolate the relationship between taxes on the poor and poverty-related outcomes, net of all the things that are relatively stable over time, such as regional variation in the cost of living.

CHANGE OVER TIME

Before presenting the results of the fixed-effects models, we want to show, graphically, how *change* in taxes on the poor in recent decades relates to *change* in key poverty-related outcomes. In this exercise we focus on three outcomes of interest: state-level age-adjusted mortality, state property crime rates, and state violent crime rates.

Ordinary least squares regressions for every state, with taxes as the outcome variable and year as the only predictor, tell us something about the relationship. The slope on the year coefficient indicates how taxes in that state have changed over time. We used the same procedure for each of the outcome variables and then graphed the relationship between the change in taxes over time (slope) and the change in the outcome of interest (slope) over time by state.

Our aim is to get a sense of whether we see a relationship between the change in taxes on the poor and the change in state-level outcomes such as mortality. Without "controlling" for any other factors, this first step in our longitudinal analysis can give us a sense of whether the states that increase taxes are the same states that experience increases in crime or, in the case of mortality—where every state sees a decrease in this period—whether states that increase taxes on the poor see a smaller decline than states that reduce the tax burden on the poor. This analysis, therefore, serves as a useful preliminary test for whether changes in taxes on the poor and state-level outcomes are correlated. More sophisticated techniques are then used to test whether this relationship is statistically significant.

MORTALITY

Chapter 3 showed that the health profile of the southern states is not encouraging. These states display high rates of infant mortality, childhood and adult obesity, heart disease, and deaths due to cerebrovascular disease and strokes. These conditions combine to produce a higher overall pattern of mortality in the region. We now estimate the relationship of taxation to mortality, adjusted to take into account the divergent age profiles of the different state populations. The x-axis in figure 17 represents change in age-adjusted mortality (the slope from the ordinary least squares regression of mortality on year by state). The y-axis is the change in taxes on the poor (the slope from the ordinary least squares regression of taxes on year by state). In both instances, we are looking at data covering the period from 1982 to 2006.

Throughout the country, patterns of mortality improved during this period. Age-adjusted mortality went down in every state. That is the good news. But the states that improved the most during this twenty-four-year period were the states that exacted the lowest tax burden from the poor, and the states with the least improvement were typically southern states that hit the poor with high taxes.

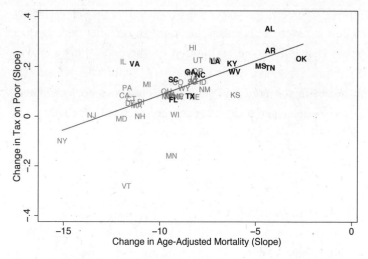

Figure 17. Change in mortality and change in tax on the poor. Southern states are in bold.

PROPERTY CRIME

The relationship between crime and the economy is controversial. Some scholars have argued that people who have few alternatives for earning a living will become more crime prone and hence there is a direct relationship between crime and poor labor market prospects. Others believe the evidence is too weak because crime can go down even when the economy tanks (as happens to be the case in 2010, with a deep recession but record-low homicide rates). To the extent there is a consensus of any kind, it seems to be that crime, especially property crime, does respond to economic distress and labor market fluctuation (figure 18).[8]

Between 1982 and 2006, the period for which we have data on property crime rates, many states saw improvement in their property crime statistics, while others went in the other direction. The states where property crime dropped the most dur-

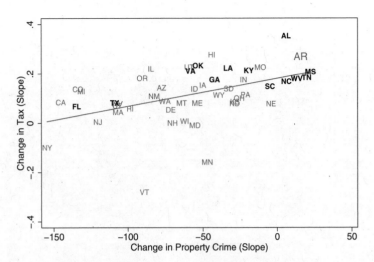

Figure 18. Change in property crime and change in tax on the poor. Southern states are in bold.

ing this period were those that held steady or even reduced the tax burden on the poor, while the states that experienced an increase in property crime were typically those southern states that increased taxes on families below the poverty line.

Violent crime is another outcome for which the experience of the states has varied, with some reducing crime and others seeing an increase between 1982 and 2006. Once again, as figure 19 indicates, the states that improved the most—that saw the steepest reduction in violent crime—were those that reduced taxes on the poor, while those that saw an increase in property crime were the states that increased taxes on the poor, especially those in the South. Although from this vantage point violent crime does not appear to be as strongly correlated with taxing the poor as mortality or property crime, more sophisticated statistical analyses are needed to determine whether the two are related.

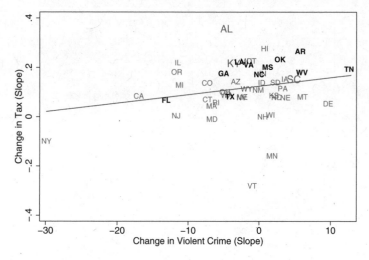

Figure 19. Change in violent crime and change in tax on the poor. Southern states are in bold.

"FIXED-EFFECTS" ANALYSES

What if individual states are just different? Different in a way that inclines those in the South to tax the poor *and* experience these bad outcomes? Even taking the slope graphs in the previous section into account, it is possible that unique characteristics of states are driving both sets of outcomes. Fixed-effects analysis lets us control for state-level characteristics that do not change over time. Still, other factors may well be changing at the state level that could be rival explanations for the relationship we observe between changes in taxes and change in poverty-related outcomes. Accordingly, we include a comprehensive set of statistical controls that will help us to eliminate the possibility that, for example, changes in the state unemployment rate or the state poverty rate are the true drivers in the relationship between taxes and outcomes.

CONTROLLING FOR COMPETING EXPLANATIONS

In the analyses that follow, we are controlling in all cases for the following variables and their fluctuations over time:[9]

Racial Composition of State (Percentage)　Social science research consistently demonstrates the salience of race in determining outcomes as varied as health, educational attainment, employment, and income. We must therefore control for the racial composition of each state. If, for example, Latinos are more likely to drop out of high school than non-Hispanic whites, a state that sees an increase in Latinos over two decades will see a lower high school completion rate, all else equal. In each of our models, we control for the percent of the population that is black and the percent Latino in each state for each year.

Poverty Rate　Our key outcomes are clearly associated with poverty. States that see an increase in poverty in this period are likely to do worse on the poverty-related outcomes we care about, regardless of the level of taxation in the state. It may be the case that states that increased the tax burden on the poor also see an increase in the poverty rate during this period; not accounting for the change in the state poverty rate might then lead us to wrongly conclude that increased taxes are the culprit. As state-level outcomes are undeniably associated with the proportion of the population in absolute poverty, we control for the state poverty rate for each year.

State GDP (per Capita)　Downturns in the business cycle can have a tremendous effect on the economic—and consequently physical and emotional—well-being of any family, especially those already in a precarious position. In a country as large and diverse as the United

States, the health of state economies can vary dramatically, especially over time, and therefore may explain state variation in our outcomes. For this reason, we control for state-level GDP per capita for each year to capture the strength of the economy in each state.

Unemployment Rate   The state unemployment rate serves as an additional indicator of the financial health of households as well as the health of the overall economy in the state. By controlling for unemployment rates by state, we are trying to ensure that we are not simply picking up the consequences of the changing dynamics of state unemployment on our outcome variables.

State Gini Coefficient   High levels of economic inequality have been shown to be associated with a number of the outcomes we test here, notably health and crime. To rule out the possibility that changing patterns of inequality within states explain our outcome measures, we include state Gini coefficients for each year as a control in our models.

State Direct Expenditure (per Capita)   All else equal, states that simply spend more—on education, public health, and public assistance programs—are likely to have very different outcomes than states that spend comparatively little. What's more, changes in our outcomes of interest are likely related to changes in state spending: states that increase their spending may post better outcomes than states that do not. For this reason we control for state direct expenditure for each year, which is a summary measure of all spending done at the state and local level.[10]

Federal Intergovernmental Revenue (per Capita)   Some federal policy changes, such as those targeted toward poor families, may affect states differently. If a federal policy shift causes Washington to send more dollars to one state capital than another, state outcomes could be disparately affected. For this reason we control for state revenue from the federal government for each year.

Before proceeding to the results of our fixed-effects analyses, two points bear mentioning. First, fixed-effects models impose very rigorous constraints and, as a result, typically knock out the kinds of findings found in standard cross-sectional analyses. But in our fixed-effects models, this turns out not to be the case for several important outcomes. The relationships between taxation on the poor and our key poverty-related outcomes are robust and statistically significant. Second, the length of time it might take for a change in taxes to affect any of the outcomes we discuss below is hard to estimate. It seems reasonable to assume that if taxes increase the cost of food and lead the poor to shift to less healthy diets, obesity might follow in fairly short order. But mortality could take many years. How do we know what the appropriate lag measure would be? The short answer is that statistically this is not an issue for our models. The long answer can be found in appendix I, written by our colleague Scott Lynch, statistician and demographer at Princeton.

THE IMPACT OF TAXING THE POOR

Table 5 displays the results of our state and year fixed-effects regression of the relationship between mortality, crime rates (property and violent crime), high school completion, and births to unmarried mothers—all outcomes that are of central concern to policy makers—and taxes on the poor. We note that the relationship between taxes on the poor and four of these five outcomes is highly significant (at the $p < .01$ level) and in the predicted direc-

Table 5

State and local taxes on the poor and poverty-related outcomes:
State and year fixed-effects regression with controls

Outcome	Years	Taxes on the poor (β)	Standard error	Overall R^2
State age-adjusted mortality rate ($N = 147$)	1982; 1990; 2005	0.0666997***	0.0122106	0.4626
State property crime rate per 100,000 ($N = 1,127$)	1982–2006	0.7828382***	0.0740552	0.0864
State violent crime rate per 100,000 ($N = 1,127$)	1982–2006	0.1233097***	0.0140618	0.2232
State high school completion rate ($N = 980$)	1982–2002	−0.0025866***	0.000761	0.2354
Births to unmarried mothers as percent of all births ($N = 735$)	1990–2006	0.0006583*	0.0003656	0.1744

NOTES: ***$p < .01$; **$p < .05$; *$p < .1$; Alaska was excluded from the analysis.
Time-variant controls included: Δ % black, Δ % Hispanic, Δ poverty rate, Δ state GDP per capita, Δ state direct expenditure, Δ unemployment, Δ federal intergovernmental revenue, Δ state Gini coefficient.

tion: an increase in taxes on the poor leads to an increase in the incidence of these social problems, accounting for all state-level characteristics that do not change over time and any changes in the control variables included in the model.[11] Moreover, our results are robust to a number of different model specifications and sensitivity analyses.[12]

The coefficient on the tax variable can be interpreted as follows: In this period, for every $100 increase in taxes on the poor, the mortality rates increased by 6.6 per 100,000. As a benchmark, we note that in 2005 the average state age-adjusted mortality rate was 802.56 per 100,000. The same dollar increase in taxes is associated with an increase in the state property crime rate of 78.3 per 100,000. For comparison, the average property crime rate across the states analyzed was 3,236.36 per 100,000 in 2006. As is the case for property crime, the magnitude of the tax coefficient is notable. It suggests that every $100 increase in taxes on the poor during this period is associated with an increase in the state violent crime rate of 12.3 per 100,000. In 2006, the average state violent crime rate was 404.43 per 100,000.

Having a high school diploma is a major predictor of a person's ability to succeed in the labor market. We saw in chapter 3 that many southern states have dropout rates well above the national average. But is there a relationship between taxes on the poor and high school completion?[13] Although the magnitude of the coefficient is quite small, the relationship between taxes and high school completion is highly significant (at the $p < .01$ level) and in the predicted direction; increasing taxes on the poor decreases high school completion rates. The coefficient indicates that for every $100 increase in taxes on the poor during this period, the state high school completion rate decreases by 0.26 percentage points. As a benchmark, in 2002 the mean high school completion rate, as calculated by John R. Warren, across all states in the analysis was approximately 73 percent.[14]

Out-of-wedlock childbearing is problematic for children and their mothers. These families have been deemed "fragile" because they are vulnerable to poverty and instability.[15] The coefficient on births to unmarried mothers is similarly very small, but we note that it is in the predicted direction, though only marginally significant (at the $p < .10$ level). Interpretation of the coefficient suggests that during this period, a $100 increase in taxes on the poor is associated with a 0.07 percentage point increase in the percentage of births to unmarried mothers. In 2006 the mean percentage of births to unmarried mothers across the states included in the analysis was 37.48.

Taken together, these analyses demonstrate that increasing taxes on the poor exacerbates the poverty-level outcomes that are of primary interest to many policy makers and social science researchers. But *how* does the way taxes treat the poor make outcomes worse? It is true, as we discuss below, that states that tax the poor also spend less on programs designed to increase the health, well-being, and mobility of poor families. But our models presented above already control for changes in the level of state spending. How then can we account for this relationship? Our argument is simple: money matters.

MONEY MATTERS

From the beginning of this volume, we have emphasized the importance of between-state (or between-region) differences in the history of tax policy. Yet our analysis of time trends has relied entirely on change within states. Can we assert that the same mechanism is at work? Can the differences within states over time—which show a clear relationship between taxing the poor and a variety of negative outcomes—be extended to account for the differences between states? We argue that the between-state differences that are so starkly displayed in chapter 3 are at least in part the consequence of tax policies that hammer the Jones family of Georgia while providing rebates to an identical Jones family in Vermont. It stands to reason that if taxing the poor produces negative outcomes within states over time, it will also do so across states.

Nonetheless, why should taxation on the poor produce these

findings at all? What is the mechanism by which taxation drives these pernicious outcomes? Why should it be that taxing the poor moves state level mortality, for example? The most likely explanation is that money matters. The impact of taxation is to deprive the poor of resources they would otherwise be able to spend, and that deprivation is more pronounced in the southern states that have practiced regressive taxation for decades than it is in the non-southern states that tend toward more progressive tax structures. The poor in the southern states, therefore, suffer on a persistent basis the loss of disposable income that would otherwise be available to them. And to the extent that money does things like enable the Jones family to buy more nutritious food and perhaps remain healthier as a result, reduce stress on single mothers so that they are calmer or more supportive parents, pay for Grandma Jones's medications and stave off her untimely passing, or leave a young man enough money to manage without committing crimes, we can infer relationships between taxation and the outcomes we have tracked. At least as far as we can see at this point, there is no other simple way to explain the pathway that leads from tax regimes to poverty-related outcomes, particularly after controlling for the other obvious culprits.

What evidence do we have that money matters in this way? After all, some prominent scholars—for example, Susan Mayer at the University of Chicago—have argued the contrary. Mayer, in particular, suggests that "money can't buy" a lot of poverty-avoiding behaviors.[16] Once children's basic material needs are met, she argues, it is the other characteristics of their parents (that are not money-reliant, like parental diligence, good health, cooperativeness) that really determine children's long-term outcomes. And what families do when they have more money in hand is buy things that don't really affect children's school success.

On the other hand, Mayer joined with Christopher Jencks in writing an important article two decades ago that points to a host of factors that are generally associated with having less money and that seem to have pernicious effects on the poor:[17] living in neighborhoods with a high concentration of other poor families, attending schools with students of a lower average socioeconomic status, or attending schools that are more racially segregated.[18] These conditions tend to lead to worse educational outcomes, which could certainly culminate in higher dropout rates. Having more money to put toward rent may also translate into lower exposure to crime or less individual motivation to commit crime, and either of those contextual differences could be responsible for differential crime rates in states with divergent tax rates for the poor.

Having less money, which is one consequence of living in a state where taxes take a bigger bite out of a family's resources, may push the poor into lower-income neighborhoods where, we know, the likelihood of having a child out of wedlock grows. David Harding[19] has shown that young men who grow up in violent neighborhoods—which are associated with poverty— are more likely to drop out of school and become teen fathers because they form age-heterogeneous social networks for protection from local thugs. Those networks expose them prematurely to sexual activity and lack of attachment to school among the older boys, who are not the most admirable role models. Having more money at the end of the month makes it more likely that poor children can escape these influences.

The amount of money that separates states that tax the poor heavily from those that provide substantial rebates is substantial: $2,300 on an income of $18,000 represents the difference between the Jones family in Vermont and their counterparts in

Alabama. Is it reasonable to expect that a difference of that magnitude will shift poverty-related outcomes in a meaningful way?

We would be on safer ground if we could demonstrate that the outcomes evident in our state fixed-effects models are also evident when taxation is not the reason why families below the poverty line are systematically cash deprived. To explore this point, we reworked our previous fixed-effects models, and instead of examining change in *taxes* on the poor, we analyzed how the change in average *income* for the bottom 20 percent of households in each state (adjusted for inflation) is associated with our outcomes of interest.

Table 6 presents the results of this analysis. The model indicates that net of prevailing characteristics of the macro economy, if the income of the poor increases, the state age-adjusted mortality rate decreases. We posit, then, that it is reasonable to think that taxes work the same way: as they increase, take-home income decreases, and this produces increased mortality. The same can be said of the relationship between the economic well-being of the bottom 20 percent of households and state property crime rates. Net of other changes in the macro economy, as the income of the poor increases, state property crime decreases. Money also seems to matter (albeit in a less powerful way) for the rate of out-of-wedlock births: as the income of the bottom quintile increases, the percent of births to unmarried mothers decreases.

These findings almost certainly *understate* the true magnitude of the impact of taxation on the poor. This is because the statistical models demonstrate the effect of taxing the poor upon the *entire population* of a given state, not just upon that state's poverty population. Our models show that states that tax the poor more have higher average mortality, for example, for their *whole* population and not specifically higher mortality among their citizens

Table 6

Mean income of bottom quintile and poverty-related outcomes:
State and year fixed-effects regression with controls

Outcome	Years	Mean income bottom quintile (β)	Standard error	Overall R^2
State age-adjusted mortality rate ($N = 147$)	1982; 1990; 2005	-0.0096608**	0.0042304	0.1425
State property crime rate per 100,000 ($N = 1,127$)	1982–2006	-0.0628026***	0.0196507	0.1034
Births to unmarried mothers as percent of all births ($N = 735$)	1990–2006	-0.0001949**	0.0000896	0.1564

NOTES: ***$p < .01$; **$p < .05$; *$p < .1$; Alaska was excluded from the analysis.
Time-variant controls included: Δ % black, Δ % Hispanic, Δ poverty rate, Δ state GDP per capita, Δ state direct expenditure, Δ unemployment, Δ federal intergovernmental revenue, Δ state Gini coefficient.

who live in poverty. Common sense would suggest, however, that the negative consequences of taxing the poor do not fall evenly across the whole of a state's population, from rich to poor. Rather, we would expect that if, as we observed, taxing the poor is associated with increased average mortality, that extra mortality would disproportionately affect the poor. Similarly, dropping out of high school and crime may be expected to be more frequent among the poor. So for those indicators, too, the average estimate measured across the state's population probably considerably understates the negative impacts on the poor themselves.[20]

To get at this question, it is critical to move away from analyses that depend on state-level outcomes and to consider how additional income (whether from earnings or tax rebates or both) moves the needle on the poverty-related outcomes *among the poor themselves.* A number of recent studies take this additional step, and the evidence they provide adds credence to the idea that when the poor either earn or are given more money, the negative outcomes diminish and positive ones grow. This seems to be the case whether the funds come as steady earnings at a higher rate, periodic windfalls, or tax rebates.

The Manpower Demonstration Research Corporation (MDRC) is well known for pioneering random-assignment evaluations of antipoverty programs. These gold standard experiments assign a treatment to one group and withhold it from a matched population in order to isolate the impact of a new policy as accurately as possible. MDRC researchers Pamela Morris and Christopher Rodrigues, working alongside University of California, Irvine, economist Greg Duncan, examined seven experiments that assigned welfare-recipient mothers at random to control groups or policy treatments that were "designed to increase employment and reduce welfare."[21] The treatments usually provided some kind of income supplement to poor, single-parent families, in part to encourage them to purchase childcare needed to keep the adults in the labor market or to pay for the cost of work clothes. Other experiments incentivized work by threatening to withhold welfare payments unless mothers remained on the job.

Whatever the form of the experiment, the data permits researchers to look at the relationship between income (earned as well as welfare payments and/or cash supplements) and children's cognitive performance or school achievement.[22] Because data were collected on children's preexperiment cognitive characteristics, it was possible to see whether or not increased income made a difference in their postexperiment performance. The conclusions fit well with the "money matters" line of thinking: "programs with the largest positive impacts on income tend to have larger positive impacts on child achievement."[23] A $1,000 increase in annual income increased the achievement of children by 6 percent of a standard deviation.

We know that poverty has its most devastating effects when it intersects the lives of young children. Do their *long-term* pathways shift in positive ways if their families experience a significant increase in income during their childhood? An interesting, if unintended, experiment in a region of North Carolina helps us to see that the answer is yes.[24] The Great Smoky Mountains Study of Youth began in 1993 and gathered longitudinal data on children.[25] Because the researchers were interested in the developmental pathways of children in poverty, they oversampled American Indians from the Eastern Band of the Cherokee.

Three years after the study began, a casino owned by the tribe opened. All adult members of the tribe were eligible to receive a portion of the profits from gambling, and starting in 1996, the funds began to flow into the households of the Cherokee to the tune of approximately $4,000 annually. This "exogenous shock" made it possible to examine the impact of increasing income on children's outcomes, and the results are impressive: at age twenty-one, children in the poorest Cherokee households saw an additional year of education, and the chances of committing a minor crime decreased by 22 percent for sixteen- and seventeen-year-olds. What was the mechanism or pathway by which the windfall affected these outcomes? Randall Akee and his colleagues argue that "improved parental quality" was the likely explanation. Parents did not reduce their work time to hang around with their kids, a competing possibility. But because they were less stressed, the timbre of their interactions with kids improved.[26]

The welfare-to-work experiments and the Great Smoky Mountain study focus on income increases that are tied to earnings or cash supplements. What if the extra money comes instead from tax rebates of the kind we have been examining in our fixed-effects models? Gordon Dahl and Lance Lochner offer a way to explore this question.[27] They examined the impact of increases in the EITC on the math and reading achievements of 5,000 children, matched to their mothers, in the National Longitudinal Survey of Youth. They found that a $1,000 increase in income generated by an increasingly generous EITC "raises combined math and reading test scores by 6% of a standard deviation in the short run" and they showed that "the gains are larger for children from disadvantaged families."[28] Indeed, their analyses suggest that black and Hispanic children, kids in single-parent households, and those born to mothers with little education show the greatest improvement in test scores as a consequence of the additional income flowing into their households through this tax credit.[29] Taken together with our own analyses on statewide outcomes of taxing the poor, we think there is good reason to believe that our results are best explained by the most straightforward relationship: money matters.

It might shed further light on the money-matters story if we knew how poor households that receive additional funds through tax rebates like the EITC make use of the extra money they get, since the average rebate comes close to approximating the difference between the take-home monies of the poor in high- and low-taxing states. Harvard sociologist Kathryn Edin and her colleagues have been tracking families that receive at least $1,000 in EITC refunds. They observe that families tend to use the windfall to pay off debts, especially credit card bills or overdue rent or utility bills, or to purchase durable goods that require a bundle of money to buy (e.g., a car or refrigerator). It seems likely that paying off debts reduces anxiety and affects health through stress.

Indeed, Edin's interviews make it clear how much relief her interviewees feel when they can cure a backlog of overdue notices.[30] Those who can clear a landlord's bill may also be less likely to face eviction or other financially induced forms of housing instability.

The Harvard team discovered that many EITC recipients use the money for additional food. We cannot tell whether it is of better quality than what they would otherwise have purchased, but Edin's findings are consonant with the findings we describe in chapter 3 that show widespread food insecurity among the poor. Clearly much more research would need to be done to trace the mechanisms that would help to explain our findings. It will need to focus on many pathways, since it is not likely that money matters in the same way for each of these outcomes. What the mechanisms have in common, though, is the impact of persistent deprivation rather than a sharp shock, for the poor of Alabama are losing out year in and year out, not just on a one-time basis.

SALES TAX ON FOOD AND OBESITY

Southern states squeeze tax revenue out of the poor, not only through high tax rates, but also by taxing basic household necessities that are exempt in most other parts of the country, notably food. Previous research has demonstrated the connection between the price of food and obesity: when faced with a limited budget, low-income families typically opt for cheaper, high-calorie, low-quality foodstuffs over relatively more expensive healthful, fresh products.[31] By increasing the cost of each item, a sales tax may lead some low-income families to consume less-healthful products in an effort to stretch their food budgets. Sales taxes on food, therefore, may be one explanation for the

Table 7

State and local sales taxes on the poor and
percentage of obese adults (1990 and 1995–2006):
State and year fixed-effects regression

Outcome	State/local sales tax coefficient	Standard error
Δ Percent of obese adults	0.00565***	0.0017881
Number of observations	536	Overall R^2: 0.4728

SOURCE: CDC, National Center for Health Statistics, Behavioral Risk Factor Surveillance System, http://apps.nccd.cdc.gov/brfss/.

NOTES: ***$p < .01$; **$p < .05$; *$p < .1$; Alaska was excluded from the analysis.

Time-variant controls included: Δ % black, Δ % Hispanic, Δ poverty rate, Δ state GDP per capita, Δ state direct expenditure, Δ unemployment, Δ federal intergovernmental revenue, Δ state Gini coefficient.

fact that obesity rates are higher in the South than in the rest of the country (explored in chapter 3).

To test this theory, we used fixed-effects regression analysis to compare change in the sales tax on the poor, which includes a tax on food in many states, with change in state obesity rates over time. We use the fixed-effects technique in order to net out everything that makes a state unique and may otherwise account for the trend (e.g., the famed fat content of traditional southern cooking). The results of our analysis are presented in table 7. Using state and year fixed effects and controlling for changes in racial composition, poverty rate, state GDP, state spending, and unemployment, we found that increasing *sales taxes* on the poor does appear to be associated with increased obesity rates. This relationship is highly significant at the $p < .01$ level. The coefficient tells us that for every $100 increase in sales taxes over this period, the state obesity rate increased by 0.57 percentage points. For comparison, in 2006, the average obesity rate across all states analyzed was 25.1 percent.

PUBLIC EXPENDITURES: CAN THEY REDRESS THE CONSEQUENCES OF REGRESSIVE TAXATION?

In theory, states that draw money from the pockets of the poor through the tax code could return it in other forms and "cure" deprivation by stepping in with other resources to make up the difference. Welfare grants, subsidized housing, public health expenditures—all of these supplements might help to close the gap that opens up because of regressive taxation. Does the state step in to create a more level playing field?

TANF Assistance

For poor families whose household heads earn little or no income, TANF—Temporary Assistance for Needy Families—provides critical cash benefits and vital income supports such as child care assistance. Under TANF, states receive a block grant from the federal government to administer their own welfare programs. States are also required to spend some of their own dollars on TANF programs or be forced to pay severe penalties to the federal government. These state "maintenance of effort" dollars are typically set at 80 percent of whatever the state was spending on welfare-related programs before 1996.[32] Neither the federal TANF block grants nor state maintenance of effort requirements have increased since the program began in 1997. According to the Center on Budget and Policy Priorities, this means that the real value of the federal block grant has declined by almost 27 percent, and the amount states spend on welfare-

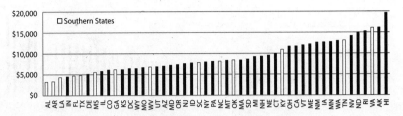

Figure 20. TANF income eligibility thresholds for a family of three, 2005.

related programs has declined by 45 percent in real terms since 1994.[33]

Even though the value of these benefits has declined drastically over time,[34] they remain vital to the poor, particularly to mothers of young children who cannot work or who earn very low wages. Eligibility for TANF varies considerably across the states. Perhaps unsurprisingly, states that practice regressive taxation also seem to be states that are very restrictive where TANF is concerned. Hence, single parents with two children who earn as little as $3,229 annually in the state of Alabama are deemed too well off to qualify for TANF. The same family could earn $11,722 in California and still be eligible (figure 20). Families that are eligible for TANF assistance may benefit considerably from the funds transferred to them if they live in generous states. But if they have the misfortune of living in a miserly one, very little will come to them in the way of a stipend (figure 21).

For example, if the Jones family lived in Mississippi, their TANF stipend would amount to $170 a month; the Jones family of California could claim $704. Are these state differences in benefits a wash when we consider the difference in the cost of living across states? No. The Council for Community and Eco-

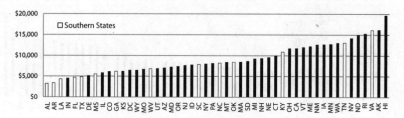

Figure 21. TANF stipend levels for a family of three, 2005.

nomic Research derived a cost-of-living index for participating cities and towns based on the costs of groceries, housing, health care, transportation, utilities, and miscellaneous expenses. Averaging indexes across cities and towns within a state yields a state cost-of-living index of 134 for California and 91.2 for Mississippi. According to this measure, the cost of living in California is 47 percent higher than in Mississippi, whereas the maximum TANF benefit is 414 percent higher in the Golden State.[35] The gap in the cost of living is therefore not sufficient to equalize the state differences in TANF benefit levels. The southern states are simply meaner and leaner: they set TANF eligibility levels far lower than the non-southern states do.

Differences between the states are also visible in the total amount of spending on TANF and the number of recipients served (table 8). The National Center for Children in Poverty has compiled data that enable us to determine the variation between states on TANF, and it is vast. In 2006, the state of Connecticut spent $124 million on 18,490 families; Mississippi spent $22 million on 13,417 families. Per capita, the southern states are relatively miserly in addressing the needs of the poor through TANF, even when correcting for differences in the cost of living.

Table 8

TANF population and spending by state, 2006

State	Adults and children receiving TANF	Total spending per recipient
Tennessee	179,985	$576
New Jersey	101,065	$769
Alabama	44,693	$774
Mississippi	27,833	$801
Arkansas	17,925	$854
Texas	160,806	$864
Indiana	119,308	$911
South Carolina	35,548	$1,083
Oklahoma	22,546	$1,229
Missouri	93,697	$1,304
Illinois	90,101	$1,371
Kansas	44,966	$1,397
Kentucky	69,928	$1,439
Delaware	12,210	$1,499
Georgia	62,584	$1,529
North Dakota	6,840	$1,535
Arizona	87,374	$1,569
West Virginia	23,726	$1,572
Pennsylvania	245,071	$1,603
District of Columbia	38,705	$1,604
North Carolina	58,801	$1,605
Montana	9,908	$1,665
Louisiana	26,749	$1,675
Colorado	37,391	$1,685
New Mexico	43,039	$1,710
Iowa	40,185	$1,839
Michigan	219,813	$1,921

(continued)

Table 8 (continued)

State	Adults and children receiving TANF	Total spending per recipient
Minnesota	66,843	$1,931
Ohio	170,195	$1,942
Florida	86,447	$1,961
South Dakota	6,093	$2,002
Utah	18,229	$2,024
Oregon	41,835	$2,118
Washington	128,323	$2,216
Maryland	46,880	$2,267
Idaho	3,054	$2,358
New Hampshire	13,742	$2,540
Nebraska	24,266	$2,609
Maine	24,814	$2,628
Nevada	12,238	$2,697
Rhode Island	23,977	$2,711
Wisconsin	39,521	$2,806
Vermont	10,946	$3,161
California	1,047,957	$3,320
Connecticut	36,841	$3,369
Massachusetts	93,379	$3,431
Alaska	9,823	$3,706
Hawaii	17,382	$4,873
Virginia	26,046	$5,210
New York	307,910	$5,274
Wyoming	509	$20,629

NOTE: TANF = Temporary Assistance for Needy Families. Southern states are shaded.

They are not alone, since other states are also on the low end, but the South clusters toward the bottom, and most of the southern states are below the national median.

Education

If a state eschews closing the tax burden gap through TANF stipends, it might nonetheless invest in public education as a means of "supporting" the poor, by making the mobility of the next generation more likely. Impatience with the adult poor, expressed through low stipends, might be redressed through greater generosity toward poor children in providing them with opportunities to enhance their human capital.

In recent years, federal expenditures on kindergarten-through-twelfth-grade education have grown, but it is still the case that the lion's share of the nation's spending on schools comes from state and local sources.[36] On average, U.S. school districts spent $8,287 per year per pupil in 2004; but the variation in spending patterns is considerable, both between states and within them. Map 24 demarcates the states in terms of their spending.

With the exception of West Virginia, *all* of the southern states fall below the national average in educational spending. A significant cluster of them—including Alabama, Florida, Kentucky, Mississippi, North Carolina, and Tennessee—fall more than 20 percent below the national average, while most of the rest are spending about $1,000 less per student than the national average. South Carolina, Georgia, Tennessee, Louisiana, Alabama, North Carolina, and Virginia all rely in part on local sales taxes to fund education; at the same time, Alabama, Tennessee, and North Carolina each rank in the bottom ten among states for per pupil expenditure, with South Carolina—ranked thirty-sixth nationally—not

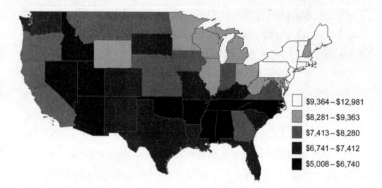

Map 24. State education spending per pupil, 2004. Source: New America Foundation, Federal Education Budget Project.

far behind in the race to the bottom.[37] This is the case even after accounting for the significant equalizing effect of federal education funding. These inequalities encourage those with means to flee public schools, as they have been doing since the nineteenth century.[38]

RUNNING A STRIPPED-DOWN STATE

States that rely on regressive taxation are invading the pocketbooks of the very citizens who can least afford to pay. But setting aside these equity questions, which are serious indeed, we should consider whether regressive taxation yields the resources necessary to support a well-functioning state. The answer is that it doesn't. Table 9 is a pooled regression with year fixed effects that examines the relationship between taxation of the poor and state direct and social expenditures per capita. It shows that those states that tax the poor heavily spend *less* overall per capita (for their poor and nonpoor citizens alike) and do less social spend-

Table 9

State and local taxes on poor and state expenditure per capita:
Pooled regression with year fixed effects

Outcome	Years	Taxes on the poor (β)	Standard error
State direct expenditure per capita ($N = 1,127$)	1982–2006	−0.6529445*	0.3620186
State social expenditure per capita ($N = 1,127$)	1982–2006	−0.4977119***	0.1828845

NOTES: ***$p < .01$; **$p < .05$; *$p < .1$; Alaska was excluded from the analysis.
Controls included: Δ % black, Δ % Hispanic, Δ poverty rate, Δ state GDP per capita, Δ unemployment.

ing than states that are more tax progressive. This is important because it suggests that whatever state governments *might* do to equalize resources for the poor—giving back with one hand what was taken by the other through regressive taxation—they do not actually do. Indeed, tax-regressive states move in exactly the wrong direction: taxing the poor more, plus spending less on social programs that might help address the gaps these tax policies create.

Would it matter if state governments increased their social expenditures in general? What if they just put more money into spending targeted at the poor? Perhaps the gap between the middle class and the poor is just too big to close by depending on public resources. Susan Mayer and Leonard Lopoo address that question in a study that examines the way in which government spending affects economic mobility between the generations. They link the Panel Study of Income Dynamics, which tracked 4,800 families beginning in 1968 and expanded to include the children in that sample when they created their own households, to the data on state spending from the U.S. Census of Governments. Their findings offer powerful evidence that spending matters for mobility in general and is especially important where the mobility of the poor are concerned: "We find greater intergenerational mobility in high-spending states compared to low-spending states.... The difference in mobility between advantaged and disadvantaged children is smaller in high-spending compared to low-spending states and . . . expenditures aimed at low-income populations increase the future income of low-income but not high-income children."[39]

Targeting spending on particular services does seem to improve specific outcomes for populations at risk: "state spending on health care has been associated with a decline in infant mortality . . . and state per pupil spending on elementary and secondary schools increases low-income . . . children's educational attainment."[40] Surely this is what social spending is for: to help citizens make the most of their lives, to add to the tax coffers the results of higher earnings as mobility kicks in, and to blunt the consequences of poverty for children who have the bad luck to be born into families without means.

CONCLUSION

The poor in the southern region are at a greater disadvantage than their counterparts in other parts of the country *because* the state and local tax burdens they face make them even poorer. A particularly pernicious driver of these differences lies in the sales taxes the poor must pay (alongside the nonpoor), especially the food taxes that many southern states and localities assess.

As our analysis of the relationship between taxation and

poverty-related outcomes shows, tax policy is making a bad situation considerably worse. Our fixed-effects models show that across time, states that increase taxes on the poor do considerably worse on aggregate measures of health (mortality) and crime (aggregate property and violent crime rates), as well as social indicators (high school completion and out-of-wedlock births).

State spending fails to close this gap, in part because the resources available to many southern states are meager. The low level of revenue generated by southern tax structures impoverishes the public sector and pushes investments in public institutions like schools below the national average, often considerably below. Not surprisingly, this contributes to low levels of human capital, which in turn render the South a less attractive region for firms requiring well-educated workers. A vicious cycle emerges in which a region saddled with an unfavorable wage structure fails to capture sufficient tax revenue to support a well-endowed system of public education and depresses the health and well-being of the population.

In short, it does matter—a lot—whether a young girl in a poor family is growing up in Alabama or Vermont. At the same time, we note that the distinctive characteristics in tax regimes that separated the South from the rest of the country are starting to crop up in other regions. The advent of supermajority rules and constitutional limits on spending in places like California has introduced similar limitations on the development of the public sector. While California moves in the direction of a majority-minority state, with a heavy concentration of immigrants who will either take their places in the great middle class or fall by the wayside and sink into poverty, we see educational expenditures nose-dive in the Golden State. Statewide test scores are following suit. While the Reconstruction era history of the South helps to explain its trajectory thereafter, we should refrain from assuming that the problems exacerbated by taxing the poor are forever confined to the region below the Mason-Dixon Line. They can emerge in other parts of the country, and they have, where tax revolts have spurred political solutions that hold social spending down. To be sure, California remains a liberal state and expresses those commitments through generous renter's credits and child care credits that keep funds flowing to the lowest-income families at a far greater rate than exists in the South. But that generosity can be reversed if progressive taxation becomes a thing of the past in the West.

CHAPTER FIVE

The Bottom Line

It is rare in the history of public policy to find examples of profound, progressive change in the financial fortunes of low-income Americans. The New Deal represents a clear triumph: public employment programs in the early 1930s shoved unemployment down from 25 percent in 1935 to 13 percent by 1936, rescuing millions of families from destitution. Social Security broke what had been a durable link between old age and poverty, ensuring that the country's elderly population would live out its sunset years at a level of comfort that, though not luxurious by any means, was a major improvement. Who would imagine that the period of 1986 to 2010, an era dominated largely by conservative politics in the nation's capital, could claim the third profound change: a sharp decline (figure 22) in the federal tax burden on the poor?

This policy triumph owes itself to an idea propelled forward in its first guise in 1973 as part of Richard Nixon's proposed Family Assistance Plan, which was to replace vital income support programs such as Medicaid and food stamps with direct cash

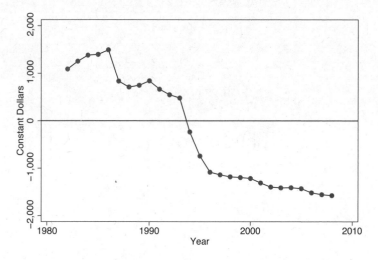

Figure 22. Federal tax liability (FICA plus income tax) for a family of three at the poverty line, 1982–2008. Source: Authors' calculations.

payments to low-income families. That proposal fell afoul of the Left and the Right and hence died an early death in Congress, but the concept of a negative income tax that would under-write the stability of the nation's poor, particularly its work-ing poor, appealed to a remarkably bipartisan group of pundits. From Daniel Patrick Moynihan to Milton Friedman, a strange set of bedfellows began a conversation about building a platform underneath the nation's poor that would ensure some degree of stability in the maelstrom of an unpredictable labor market. In 1975, the first Earned Income Credit was finally approved.[1] With the enthusiastic support of Ronald Reagan, another presi-dent rarely remembered as a friend to the poor, its successor, the Earned Income Tax Credit (EITC), expanded dramatically in 1986 and increased in 1990, 1993, and 2001. It remains one of the most important and successful antipoverty devices ever devel-

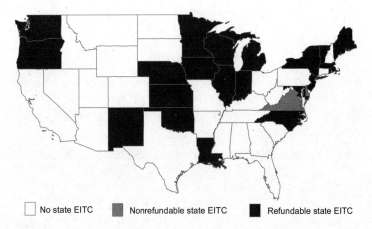

Map 25. State Earned Income Tax Credits, 2009. Source: Center on Budget and Policy Priorities.

oped. The EITC has been responsible for putting millions of dollars into the hands of the nation's most needy families.

These changes were, by definition, nationwide. The federal EITC did just as much for the poor in Mississippi as it did for the poor in Maine. But the common experience of poor Americans stops here because the states did not uniformly follow the lead of the federal government. Map 25 displays the states that have enacted their own EITCs.

The absence of most of the southern and western states is notable, though some states, like California, achieved similar results by relying on a different set of credits (e.g., renter's credits or child tax credits). Among the southern states, only Oklahoma, Louisiana, Virginia, and North Carolina had state-level EITCs as of 2009. Louisiana and North Carolina set their state benefits at 3.5 percent of the federal EITC, making theirs among the least

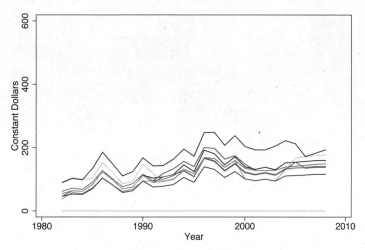

Figure 23. State and local sales tax liability for a family of three at the poverty line, northeastern states, 1982–2008. Each line represents a different state in the Northeast. Source: Authors' calculations.

generous state EITCs in the country. By contrast, New York set its state benefit at 30 percent of the federal EITC, and Wisconsin provides a benefit equal to 43 percent of the federal EITC for families with three children. But the southern states that have at least enacted earned income tax credits are more generous than the other southern states (Georgia, Alabama, Mississippi, Arkansas, Kentucky, and West Virginia) that continue to exact the whole income tax burden from the neediest households.

At the same time that the regions were moving away from one another in this aspect of tax policy, they were also diverging with respect to state and local sales taxes. Figure 23 displays the state and local sales tax liability of a family like the Joneses, a parent with two dependent children whose income is at the federal poverty line, in the Northeast.

Over the past twenty-six years, the northeastern region has

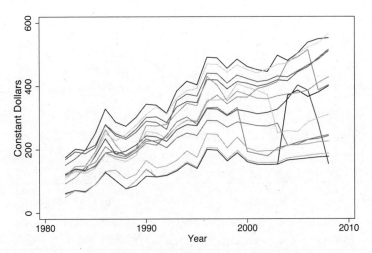

Figure 24. State and local sales tax liability for a family of three at the poverty line, southern states, 1982–2008. Each line represents a different state in the southern region. Source: Authors' calculations.

barely budged in the state and local taxes that it levies on poor households. Contrast this pattern to the increase in consumption taxes in the southern states (figure 24).

The tilt is unmistakable: the southern states have ratcheted up the sales tax liability of their poorest households during the period when the northeast has held it flat. Toward the end of this decade, some of the southern states reversed course, mainly by eliminating or reducing the food tax, which is all to the good. But overall, as figure 25 makes clear, the South stands out for its trend toward increasing the burden on the poor.

A similar divergence in regional taxation trajectories is visible in state income taxes. The northeastern states, in particular, have cut the income tax for families at the poverty line rather drastically. The sharp downward slope, with the curve well below the zero line (figure 26), reflects the introduction of state-level

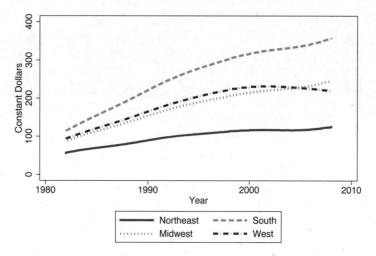

Figure 25. State and local sales tax liability for a family of three at the poverty line, by region 1982–2008. Source: Authors' calculations.

EITCs that translate into dollars in the pockets of working poor families, rather than just zeroing out their tax liabilities. Consider now the trajectory of state income taxes for poor families in the South over the same period (figure 27). Some lines are flat, and a few have reversed course, bringing the liability to zero. But not a single southern state cuts rebate checks to poor families for state income tax.

Summarizing across all regions (figure 28), we see that the North and the Midwest have lowered the income tax burden; the West has held flat. The South has crept upward very slightly, mainly because so few southern states provide for EITCs.

When we put all of the tax trajectories together—summing across state and local sales and income taxes—the stark differences between the regions of the country in their treatment of the poor become clear (figure 29).

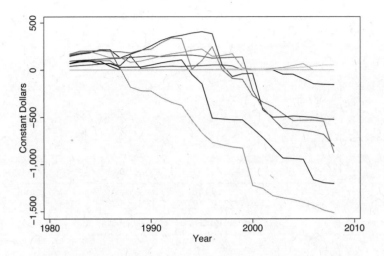

Figure 26. State income tax liability for a family of three at the poverty line, northeastern states, 1982–2008. Each line represents a different state in the Northeast.

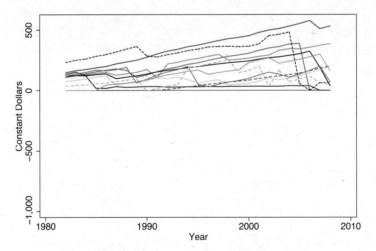

Figure 27. State income tax liability for a family of three at the poverty line, southern states, 1982–2008. Each line represents a different state in the southern region.

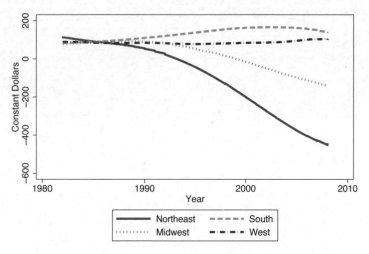

Figure 28. State income tax liability for a family of three at the poverty line, by region 1982–2008. Source: Authors' calculations.

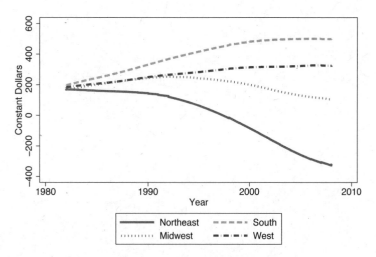

Figure 29. Total state and local tax liability for a family of three at the poverty line, by region 1982–2008. Source: Authors' calculations.

SOUTHERN DEPENDENCY

As we noted in chapter 2, over the last quarter century, state spending has increased dramatically, more than doubling in many states even after adjusting for inflation. The regions of the country are moving in tandem, with the rate of increase only slightly higher in the Northeast than in the rest of the country. Much of this increase in spending has been on social programs, including health, education, and public welfare. Federal spending has similarly increased, and with it, heavy matching burdens for states, especially in programs such as Medicaid and unfunded mandates that require states to meet funding commitments without additional help (figure 30).

Where, then, do the states find the money to meet these spending/matching requirements?

Figure 31 displays the mix of revenues that the regions of the country relied on in 2006 for supporting state expenditures. The Northeast depends heavily on property taxes, as does the Midwest; in general, property taxes are progressive, since they exact a toll only on those wealthy enough to own property and hit hardest those who have the most. Income tax is similarly progressive, though the bite differs from state to state according to the rates for different income groups. What is striking in this comparison is the reliance on sales tax: here the South stands out for the gap between the proportion of its state revenue that comes from this regressive source and the other elements in its "tax basket." The western region also draws more from sales tax than it does from property tax. But as we saw in chapter 2, this difference is of more recent vintage and reflects the pressure that supermajority requirements and tax limits, stemming from the tax revolts of the 1970s—including California's Proposition 13—

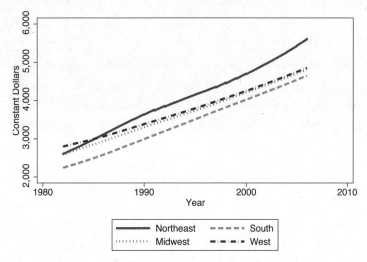

Figure 30. Total state and local social expenditure per capita, by region 1982–2008. Source: Authors' calculations.

have exerted over time to hold down property tax. In this it resembles the South, which got a head start in discouraging tax increases, leaving the sales tax as the most politically feasible avenue to use to meet state financial obligations.

Some political figures have argued that sales taxes are fair—and should be used often—because they cost consumers the same amount for the same purchases. Conservative states are not the only entities that rely on consumption taxes—far from it. Many of the social democracies of Europe rely far more heavily on consumption taxes—like the value-added tax—than on income taxes for the revenue they need to fund highly redistributive welfare states. This is clearly not the outcome we see in most of the U.S. states that rely on sales tax. On the contrary, states that tax the poor are also those that spend the least on them. But there

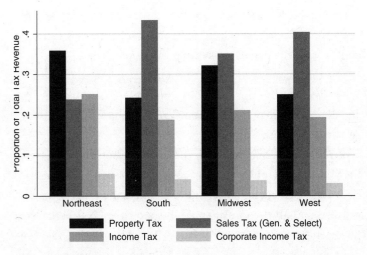

Figure 31. Total state and local tax revenue by source, 2006. Source: U.S. Census Bureau, *2007 Census of Governments.*

are other reasons why that relationship holds, besides the fact that raising revenue in this fashion doesn't actually generate a lot of treasure for the state treasury. Other alternatives are under-exploited. A brief examination of them makes it clear why—apart from the impact of procedural barriers and voting hurdles—the South ends up relying on sales tax. It isn't just the mix of tax sources that matter: it is the rate at which the alternative sources are set.

MISSING SOURCES?
PROPERTY AND CORPORATE INCOME TAX

For most states, property taxes are essential to the quality of public sector services—schools, police and fire departments, municipal facilities like swimming pools, city parks, garbage collection, and other essential services. But states and localities can only deliver what the public purse can provide for.

On that score, we know (from chapter 1) that the southern states historically went easy on property tax (and income tax) and derived more of their revenue from sales taxes. Table 10 suggests the tradition continues.

Eight of the ten states with the lowest property taxes are in the Old South. Only Virginia, Florida, and Texas crack the barrier of the median, and even there, the median property tax rate is less than half the rate charged in states like New York, New Jersey, or (traditionally conservative) New Hampshire. The consequences for the public sector could not be more profound. Lacking a property tax base to draw upon to fund essential services, the southern states must turn elsewhere to support the public sector.

Corporate tax rates vary considerably from state to state. If we sort by top corporate income tax bracket (map 26), we find southern states have, on average, relatively low ceilings on this source of revenue, and every southern state save Louisiana is in the bottom half of the states nationwide. They are not alone in being low-corporate-tax states, but they are among the more heavily populated states that are kind to business.

Table 11 is a pooled regression with year fixed-effects that shows that states that tax the poor are also states that raise less property and corporate tax revenue per capita.

Under-reliance on property tax and corporate tax leaves the states that follow this path with a revenue gap that has to be filled somehow. One of the fillers seems to involve higher taxes on the poor, particularly through sales taxes. But that is not the only avenue available to support public expenditures.

Table 10

Property tax burdens by state, 2006

State	Median tax	Median value	Tax as percentage of home value
Louisiana	$175	$101,700	0.17%
Alabama	$302	$97,500	0.31%
West Virginia	$389	$84,400	0.46%
Mississippi	$416	$82,700	0.50%
Arkansas	$459	$87,400	0.53%
Oklahoma	$635	$89,100	0.71%
South Carolina	$642	$113,100	0.57%
Kentucky	$693	$103,900	0.67%
New Mexico	$707	$125,500	0.56%
Wyoming	$737	$135,000	0.55%
Tennessee	$794	$114,000	0.70%
Delaware	$806	$203,800	0.40%
Hawaii	$924	$453,600	0.20%
North Carolina	$966	$127,600	0.76%
Missouri	$1,012	$123,100	0.82%
Georgia	$1,050	$147,500	0.71%
Indiana	$1,079	$114,400	0.94%
Utah	$1,130	$167,200	0.68%
Arizona	$1,133	$185,400	0.61%
Idaho	$1,226	$134,900	0.91%
Colorado	$1,297	$223,300	0.58%
Montana	$1,309	$131,600	0.99%
North Dakota	$1,326	$88,600	1.50%
Kansas	$1,337	$107,800	1.24%
Iowa	$1,355	$106,600	1.27%
South Dakota	$1,404	$101,700	1.38%
Virginia	$1,418	$212,300	0.67%
Nevada	$1,445	$283,400	0.51%

(continued)

Table 10 (continued)

State	Median tax	Median value	Tax as percentage of home value
Florida	$1,495	$189,500	0.79%
Ohio	$1,598	$129,600	1.23%
Minnesota	$1,618	$198,800	0.81%
Maine	$1,742	$155,300	1.12%
Michigan	$1,846	$149,300	1.24%
Nebraska	$1,889	$113,200	1.67%
Oregon	$1,910	$201,200	0.95%
Texas	$1,926	$106,000	1.82%
Pennsylvania	$1,937	$131,900	1.47%
Maryland	$2,159	$280,200	0.77%
Alaska	$2,241	$197,100	1.14%
Washington	$2,250	$227,700	0.99%
California	$2,278	$477,700	0.48%
Wisconsin	$2,777	$152,600	1.82%
Vermont	$2,835	$173,400	1.63%
Illinois	$2,904	$183,900	1.58%
Massachusetts	$2,974	$361,500	0.82%
Rhode Island	$3,071	$281,300	1.09%
New York	$3,076	$258,900	1.19%
Connecticut	$3,865	$271,500	1.42%
New Hampshire	$3,920	$240,100	1.63%
New Jersey	$5,352	$333,900	1.60%

NOTE: Southern states are shaded.

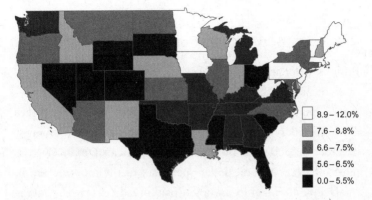

	8.9 – 12.0%
	7.6 – 8.8%
	6.6 – 7.5%
	5.6 – 6.5%
	0.0 – 5.5%

Map 26. Top state corporate income tax rate, 2009. Source: Tax Foundation.

Table 11

State and local tax revenue per capita and taxes on the poor:
State and year fixed-effects regression with controls

Outcome	Years	Taxes on the poor (β)	Adj. standard error
State/local property tax revenue per capita (N = 1,127)	1982–2006	−0.5192214***	0.130583
State/local corporate tax revenue per capita (N = 1,127)	1982–2006	−0.0530029*	0.0298402

NOTES: ***p < .01; **p < .05; *p < .1; Alaska was excluded from the analysis.
Time-variant controls included: Δ % black, Δ % Hispanic, Δ poverty rate,
Δ state GDP per capita, Δ unemployment.

FEDERAL INTERVENTION:
HOW MUCH GOOD DOES IT DO?

Billions of dollars flow from Washington to the states in the form of Medicaid matching funds, welfare block grants, disability payments, food stamps, and housing assistance. As map 27 makes clear, the federal government spends variable amounts of money, different in each state. But if we look at which states receive the most for every federal dollar spent, six of the top nine are in the Deep South. For every dollar paid in federal taxes by southern citizens, they receive, on average, $1.40 in funding from the federal government. Contrast this "match" to the ratio of dollars paid and dollars received by other states, and the "southern problem" becomes even starker: New York state receives only $0.79 of every dollar paid in taxes, California only $0.78. Of all southern states, only Florida and Texas pay more in federal taxes than they receive in federal funding, at a return rate of $0.97 and $0.94 per dollar, respectively. The nation is subsidizing low-wage employers in the southern states, who face less wage pressure as a result. This is partly because the federal government is pouring money into the region, not least through large investments in military bases. But it is also because the federal government is putting more money into poverty relief in the South in order to close a huge gap created, in part, by the unwillingness of the states to fund poverty relief themselves.

This is not a recent development; the regional divergence has been *growing* over time. Just as the South has been collecting more from its poor citizens, it has also been asking for (and receiving) more from the federal government. The Northeast began losing out on its share of federal revenue in the mid 1980s and has flatlined ever since. The Midwest has increased its take of fed-

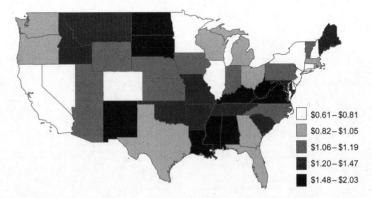

Map 27. Federal spending per dollar of federal taxes paid, 2005. Source: Tax Foundation.

eral dollars, albeit at a slower rate than the South, and the West has fluctuated over time but has fundamentally come back to the same level it had in the early 1980s. But the ratio of return of federal dollars received to state contributions has risen more sharply over time for the South than for any other part of the country.

To summarize this forest of figures, we offer the following: relative to the rest of the country, the South has increasingly burdened those poor citizens least able to afford a big tax bite, using state income and sales taxes to do so. The strategy does not work well to generate income: it leaves the South with fewer dollars to work with to address an outsized problem and, plainly, it cannot manage the need. Accordingly, more than any other region, the South turns to the federal government. It exacts an enormous price in federal dollars that are flowing into a region that is both needy and, it would seem, unwilling to tax its own citizens to deal with the problem.

That cost has ballooned over the past thirty years. In 1982 the federal government distributed to the southern states $1.13

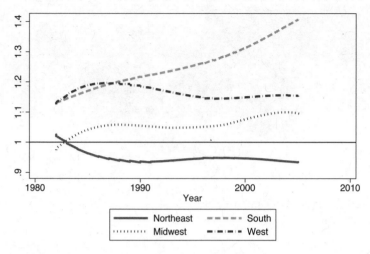

Figure 32. Federal spending per dollar of federal taxes paid, by region 1982–2005. Source: Tax Foundation.

for every dollar they paid in; it now sends back $1.40. During the same period, spending in the Northeast fell, from $1.04 for every dollar in taxes paid to Washington in 1982 to an average of just 93 cents in 2005 (figure 32).[2]

THE HUMAN AND SOCIAL COSTS
OF REGRESSIVE TAXATION

In chapter 4, we showed how regressive taxation was directly related to a series of outcomes that can be regarded only as damaging. It plays a role in early mortality, dropping out of high school, out-of-wedlock births, and crime rates (for property and violent crime). Over time, the more the poor are taxed, the worse these outcomes look within states, and this, we argue, helps to account for the regional differences in poverty-related outcomes.

Suppose Mississippi enacted tax policies that made it look

more like Massachusetts. Or: what if the southern states merely came up to the national average in state and local income and sales taxes? What kind of impact would we see on mortality or crime? The magnitude of the effects is not enormous, and we should be cautious in making claims about how different the southern world would be if it looked more like the median state. Nonetheless, the impact is not zero. So how much of a difference would it make?

The gold standard technique for isolating the impact of a change, such as the tax liability of the poor, on outcomes like mortality, crime, or family formation is to design an experiment that would take two matched groups and assign one a low tax burden and the other a high tax burden. The effect of taxation, then, could be found by comparing the outcomes of the "treated" group with the "control" group. When done properly, experiments such as these provide powerful evidence for both the presence of an effect and its magnitude.

For example, Nobel Prize–winning economist James Heckman makes a compelling case for the need for increased investment in early childhood interventions. The best evidence in support of his position rests on a handful of small-scale experiments, most notably the Perry Preschool program. Conducted in Ypsilanti, Michigan, from 1962 to 1967, the Perry Preschool randomly assigned 123 African American children between the ages of three and four from high-risk backgrounds to a "program" group that received intensive intervention or to a control group that received no intervention. Both groups were tracked for decades, and the results are remarkable: at age forty, individuals in the program/treatment group were less likely to have committed a crime and were more likely to have finished high school and be employed than individuals in the control group.

Heckman argues that early childhood interventions of this kind help children develop what he calls "noncognitive" skills that help them succeed in education and the labor market, and he estimates the return to society on the investment in early childhood intervention to be $8.70 for every dollar spent on the program, mostly due to lower criminal activity and higher employment rates of program participants.[3]

Given the logistical and ethical considerations, true experiments such as the Perry Preschool program are relatively rare in social science. However, statistical techniques, such as the fixed-effects models presented in the previous chapter, offer one way to simulate experimental conditions. By controlling for state characteristics, we are able to isolate the direct impact of taxation. The coefficient on the tax variable tells us the impact of taxes on the outcome of interest *holding all else equal.* The models therefore enable us to simulate what would happen to mortality, crime, and educational attainment if the South had eschewed their regressive policies and adopted the same tax pattern as most of the country, or the even more progressive example of the northeastern states, over the last twenty-five years.

Using the results from the fixed-effects models presented in chapter 4, this what-if scenario can be modeled in two ways: For the first, we calculated the average tax burden for all southern states and then for all non-southern states over the time period represented in our outcome variables. Second, to present a different kind of comparison, we looked at the average tax burden in the most generous region—the Northeast—over the same time period. We then calculated the difference between the average tax burden in the South and the average tax burden in the non-South (or the Northeast). Finally, we simply multiplied this difference in the tax burden by the tax coefficient from our fixed-

Table 12

Simulating the impact of different tax structures

	Coefficient from fixed-effects model	Difference of South and average tax	Additional change on outcome (per 100,000)
Mortality (1982–2005)			
All non-South	0.067	$201.08	−13.41
Northeast		$336.80	−22.46
Property crime (1982–2006)			
All non-South	0.783	$210.66	−164.91
Northeast		$354.89	−277.82
Violent crime (1982–2006)			
All non-South	0.123	$210.66	−25.98
Northeast		$354.89	−43.76

effects models. The result tells us how much better the South would look if it had adopted the mean non-South tax liability, or the mean tax liability in the Northeast, and changed nothing else (table 12).[4]

MORTALITY

Between 1982 and 2005, the average tax burden for a family of three at the poverty line in the South was $382.24 compared with $181.16 in the rest of the country, a difference of $201.08. If we multiply that number by the tax coefficient in our fixed-effects model for mortality from chapter 4, we get 201.08 × 0.067 = -13.47. This means that, had the South taxed the poor at the same rate as the rest of the country—and changed nothing else—state-level, age-adjusted mortality would have declined an additional 13.47 per 100,000 in the southern states. Suppose, instead, the southern states adopted the same tax rates as the liberal northeastern region. In that case, the difference between the actual age-adjusted mortality rate and this dream scenario would be even greater: 22.46 per 100,000.[5]

Is this a substantial difference? In 2005, the average state-level age-adjusted mortality in the South was 909.35 per 100,000. If the mortality rate declined by 18 per 100,000 (the midpoint between the most dramatic improvements, produced by using the tax rates of the Northeast, and the most mundane, using the tax rates of all states outside of the South), the change would create a 2 percent improvement.

PROPERTY CRIME AND VIOLENT CRIME

Using the same approach, we found that, had the South taxed the poor at the same rate as the rest of the country—and changed nothing else—state property crime rates would have declined an additional 165 per 100,000 in the southern states. The difference would have been even greater if the southern states had adopted the tax rates of the Northeast: 278 per 100,000. For reference, in 2006 the average property crime rate across all states was 3,236 per 100,000. Violent crime would have declined by an additional 26 (or 45 if the northeastern model was in use) per 100,000. In 2006 the average violent crime rate across all states was 404.4 per 100,000.

Is this a substantial difference? In 2006, the average state property crime rate in the South was 3,628.764 per 100,000. If the property crime rate declined by 223 per 100,000 (roughly the midpoint between the most dramatic improvement, produced by using the tax rates of the Northeast, and the most mundane, using the tax rates of all states outside of the South), the change would create a

6.8 percent improvement. In 2006, the average state violent crime rate in the South was 499.71 per 100,000. If the violent crime rate declined by 36 per 100,000 (roughly the midpoint between the most dramatic improvement, produced by using the tax rates of the Northeast, and the most mundane, using the tax rates of all states outside of the South), the change would create a 13.9 percent improvement.

These are not revolutionary differences, but they would certainly be considered moves in the right direction. Indeed, the knock-on consequences of avoiding the costs of incarceration and the loss of property and well-being for victims of crime, not to mention the many additional years of productive labor from those presently dying younger than they should, are reason enough to take these suggestions seriously.

Our other outcomes do not show effects of the same magnitude; far from it. *Very* small improvements in births to unmarried mothers (one-third of a percentage point lower) and high school completion (three-fourths of a percentage point higher) would follow if the South somehow adopted a tax structure like the most liberal part of the country, the Northeast.[6]

CONCLUSION

We titled this chapter "The Bottom Line" because we want to draw attention to the ways in which the tax regimes in the different regions of the United States continue to evolve in divergent directions. To get to that bottom line, we have looked carefully at the major elements in the tax basket and have seen how different the states are in the rates they charge the poor and the mix of taxes they rely on to support the public sector.

This is not just a problem from the distant past. In many ways, state tax policies that influence the lives of the poor were more alike in 1982 than they are now. This is not a healthy state of affairs for poor families in the southern region. They are asked to pay the highest tax burden in the country for families of their size and income; the states they live in spend the least on services that might make a difference in their lives. While the federal government, headed by Republican leaders for most of the period we are concerned with here, cut the federal burden on the poor, the southern states moved in the opposite direction. The result on the bottom line is that it matters greatly where the Jones girl is growing up. If she is in Selma, her family has seen its take-home pay decline, while her cousin in Harlem has seen it grow—by nearly $1,000.

This is not just an issue for southern citizens. The tax regime their states rely on does not bring in enough money to pay the public's bills. Accordingly, more than any other part of the country, the South turns to the federal government. And it receives much more than the rest of the country compared to what it puts in. That makes southern dependency a problem for all of us.

Are We Our Brothers' Keepers?

When the West German state threw in its lot with its Eastern cousin, it embraced a common heritage. An enormous fiscal cost was shouldered in the name of that unity. And while some voices counseled against it, the unification of Germany was a long-hoped-for dream for millions. Americans recognize the same kind of commitment to the people who inhabit the many regions of our country. We fought a civil war over the question of unity, and if there was any resolution to come out of it—as President Lincoln reminded his contemporaries in his most memorable speeches—it was that we are tied to one another in a bond that should never be broken.

In the modern era, our federal social policies are the material expression of that national solidarity. Federalism is more than a marriage of convenience that links California to Maryland or Maine to South Carolina. When tax dollars move to Washington and are released to Mississippi, we are attempting to ensure that all Americans have a fighting chance at a full and healthy life. That is what we are paying for.

To be sure, there are limits. Relative to our peers in the wealthy countries of the world, we are miserly in our assistance to the able-bodied poor. Even the catastrophe of the Great Depression provoked mean-spirited reactions; there is ample evidence in the historical trail of public opinion that Americans were suspicious of the needy and blamed them for their plight.[1] Those moral blind spots in our culture especially attach to individuals who are seen as the authors of their own misfortune. Among the most ideologically inspired, blame often attaches to entire groups of the "undeserving." But nowhere in our modern policy history is there support for the idea that a child growing up in Mobile, Alabama, or Milpitas, California, should start three steps behind a similar kid living in Milton, Massachusetts. Yet the playing field is severely tilted.

If that gap were merely a consequence of the differences in labor markets that create more opportunity for the Milton family than the one in Mobile, we would think that unfortunate and worthy of corrective action. But when the difference is a function of state policy, of the regressive taxation of those in Mobile and refundable tax credits in Milton, we have to look at the problem anew. And when we discover that this is not a lost artifact of nineteenth-century history but instead represents policy trajectories that have been diverging more sharply in the past thirty years, we have to ask harder questions.

There are some serious normative issues—with significant material implications—at stake here. Whose responsibility is it to address the needs of the poor in particular places? Clearly all taxpayers are obligated to help, which is why we have a redistributive social policy (meager as it may be when compared, for example, to the Nordic countries). But we also expect citizens of each state to provide certain kinds of support, and here the burdens are not shared equally. What do the more affluent households of the southern states owe the poor of their own region? If the tax policies of these states are lowering the longevity of their people, encouraging out-of-wedlock pregnancy (which is a poverty trap for millions), subjecting households to more crime, and impeding the accumulation of human capital, hard questions need to be asked about their responsibilities to do more, to do better. The failure to step up to that plate is placing burdens on the whole country: national resources that could be put toward other purposes are redirected to the southern states in order to patch up—however inadequately—a poverty regime that should be redressed locally as well.

How likely is it that this will come to pass? As we noted in chapter 2, the political history of the south has left deep tracks that make change extremely difficult, a barrier that became clear enough to then Governor Clinton when he attempted to reform Arkansas's tax policy in ways that would have reduced the burden on the poor and increased revenue for the state's schools. In the end, supermajority rules meant that the only revenue-raising option was the sales tax, and hence that is the instrument he turned to. The problem is not unique to the South. California has been strangling on the supermajority rules embedded in Proposition 13 and has been forced into equally unpalatable solutions, with similar consequences: the poor are in much worse shape now in the Golden State than they were before the passage of the Jarvis-Gann amendment. California's public schools once led the nation and now bring up the rear, both in revenue per pupil and in measures of quality.

Reliance on regressive taxation, undergirded by supermajority rules and limits on taxation and spending, has hammered the poor by taking money from the pockets that can least afford it.

And because it brings in relatively little, regressive taxation strips the states that run in this direction of the revenue they need to run first-class institutions that could potentially equalize, or at least take a stab at improving, the public services that could help to support better life chances for the poor. Sister Pat Flass, whose order of nuns helps to run the after-school program in the Quarters (see the Preface), could detail dozens of ways in which the low level of funding for the area schools disadvantages the poor, black children of this hamlet: "The books are worn; they are old, they have been used for years . . . and they don't have enough money to buy a lot of good books. The kids here get a list of things they have to bring to school on the first day of the year, and it includes things like toilet paper, Kleenex, and hand sanitizers. Not just school supplies, basic supplies! Because the schools can't afford . . . paper towels and toilet paper. That's pretty sad."

The teachers are poorly paid, she noted, especially in the rural areas. People with talent "don't hang around long."

Yet this strategy is self-defeating. It is costing these states more every year in lives lost prematurely, young people descending into poverty in greater numbers than they should, and crime, which takes a toll on everyone. It will take a monumental effort to change course and place the South on a trajectory that is less dependent on the federal government and better able to support the infrastructure and human capital requirements of its citizens. The cost of doing otherwise is simply too high for the people of the southern states, and it may become so in the West as well.

NEW DIRECTIONS

Few topics excite as much controversy and resistance as tax policy. In dozens of opinion polls, Americans claim that they want to see the country devote more resources to education, believe that everyone deserves health insurance, would support greater investment in public works, and think that we should do everything possible to see to it that the able bodied have jobs. But when it comes to paying for government programs that would move us toward those goals, they balk. We want it both ways: more services, more security, and lower taxes—or at least not higher taxes.

Progressive social scientists who have been thinking hard about how to square this circle have offered a number of suggestions. Among the most thoughtful is Andrea Campbell, political scientist at the Massachusetts Institute of Technology. In a paper prepared for the newly created Scholars Strategy Network,[2] a group of academics advancing innovative ideas in public policy, Campbell looks back to the experience of our most successful and durable social policy experiment—Social Security—to derive lessons for how we might change course today. She points to a number of features that made that program the third rail it is today. First, following a point made years before by Theda Skocpol,[3] the program is universal rather than means-tested and redistributive without being obvious about who wins more and who wins less (no one loses). Second, Campbell notes, paying for social security is procedurally simple and, unlike property tax, it never requires a large (irritating) lump-sum payment.[4] It is assessed gradually and is therefore less painful. Third, the tax is dedicated: it pays only for one vital program, and hence the connection between the dollars that go in and the benefits that go out is clear. We know what we are paying for and we approve of the purpose. These features have ensured a degree of popularity that is almost unmatched in the annals of American social policy.

Recognizing that we must find ways to raise revenue to invest in critical social needs and move away from deficit spending (outside of economic downturns, where a deficit-based stimulus makes sense), Campbell argues that we should consider value-added taxes (VATs). European governments have long made use of VATs, assessed on goods at the point of purchase, and they have encountered little resistance when they rely on these sales taxes to fill the government coffers.

VATs meet some of the objectives Campbell outlines: They are assessed in bits and pieces, rather than as a lump sum, so they are not "painful." Because they are used to fuel a broad social safety net, which benefits all Brits or all Germans, they are accepted in Europe and raise little ire. The revenue they bring in is redistributed in a progressive fashion through means-tested benefits, but they reach virtually all citizens to some degree. For this reason, she argues, VATs may be the way to go in the United States as well. But aren't VATs as regressive as any other sales tax? Yes, but Campbell argues that this problem can be corrected on the redistribution side: the poor will get more out of the social safety net that VATs pay for. Alternatively, as Yale law scholar—and VAT enthusiast—Michael Graetz notes, we could provide rebates on VATs to taxpayers earning less than $100,000 and thereby exempt them from its sting.

Larry Jacobs, political scientist at the University of Minnesota, concurs with Campbell and in a related paper for the Scholars Strategy Network suggests that such a plan could be framed in virtuous terms: that it will enable us to "pay our bills," acting responsibly to fund the core functions of government. He is looking for a way to trump conservative views that argue we should balance the books by cutting social spending. Instead, Jacobs says we need to raise the revenue side and sees a VAT as one way to get there.[5] The case for such a move lies, in part, in the failures of progressive income taxes, which, Jacobs points out, are unstable as a revenue source—because the rates bounce around, as a consequence of political battles over who should pay the nation's tax bill, and because they excite conservative opposition, which tends to drive spending down rather than revenue up.

We accept the propositions that Americans will not support taxes they cannot clearly identify as serving a worthy purpose and that what is valuable to them are resources they need: schools, fire departments, health care, police departments, libraries, and the like. It helps if the services in question matter over the life course; the elderly often reject school bond issues because they no longer have children young enough to need educating. But ideally, everyone gets old; everyone needs to go to the doctor or fill prescriptions; a house fire could happen to anyone. Sadly, Americans are not all that enthusiastic about being brothers' keepers. But can we rely on the notion that spending will be progressive enough to offset the financial pressures that sales taxes place on those who can least afford them?

We would surely be in safer hands if that taxing authority for VATs was the federal government, something that has never been tried. But we caution those who would solve the nation's deficit problems through regressive taxation, because there is no real guarantee that either the $100,000 threshold advocated by Graetz or the progressive spending hoped for by Campbell and Jacobs would come to pass. Granted, the recent history of the federal Earned Income Tax Credit (EITC) suggests greater largesse toward the poor at the federal level. But that policy was brought into being by lowering tax rates on the working poor, not by increasing expenditures on them. And while that might add up to the same impact on the bottom line, the politics of spending are not the same as the politics of taxing. Incentives to work are politically popular and resonate with our most enduring national values, particularly in the context of dismantling the nearly universally disliked Aid to Families with Dependent Children (AFDC) program. In the present moment, the desire to use additional revenues—if indeed they could be gathered—to pay down the national debt would be almost irresistible.

We don't believe the guarantee of progressive spending as an antidote to new consumption taxes is ironclad enough. And the experiences of the southern poor, who have borne the brunt of regressive consumption taxes for decades, should remind us of what it would mean to enact a national tax and not see its consequences reversed by refunds and/or spending. In April of 2010, the Center on Budget and Policy Priorities reported that a host of states had decided to roll back tax benefits for the poor in response to their dire fiscal conditions:

- Virginia enacted a cut in its EITC that would raise taxes by $6 million on an estimated one hundred and fourteen thousand low-income working families.
- Minnesota cut back a renter's credit affecting three hundred thousand low- and moderate-income households and eliminated a gas tax credit.
- Georgia is considering eliminating $22 million in wage support for a million workers earning less than $20,000 per year.

Similar measures have been proposed in New Jersey, the District of Columbia, and Montgomery County, Maryland.[6] To add to the problems of the poor, we find many states increasing fees for everything from driver's licenses to bridge tolls. The poor pay more, as a proportion of their income, when they make use of services of this kind. The combination of increasing fees and the rolling back of provisions that gave poor families a break on taxes is creating more hardship at precisely the time when incomes are falling.

We acknowledge that millions of Americans find sales taxes appealing and that the politics of electioneering make it a desirable possibility. The attractiveness of sales taxes emanates in part from the belief that they are fair. After all, if we have to pay an additional 10 percent on food, then all of us will face this burden on the same footing; we could always choose not to spend. Or could we? This argument makes little sense where the poor are concerned. At least 90 percent of their income is spent on necessities that they cannot "decide" to avoid. Rent, utilities, food, and clothing—these are not luxury items; they constitute the lion's share of the consumption basket for the nation's low-income households. A far higher proportion of their income disappears in consumption taxes than does from wealthy households, which can decide not to buy that yacht. Indeed, every one of the Alabama residents we interviewed was keenly aware of what taxes cost them. Alicia and Bea plan their shopping excursions around them, trying, when they can, to get to counties where the local taxes are lower for purchases. These are not trivial costs for them.

What, then, are the alternatives? We offer two different ways of thinking about policy directions. One emphasizes redressing some of the most regressive aspects of existing sales tax, without contemplating its elimination. The other takes into account the challenge of reversing course at the state level and hence focuses instead on reducing the influence of states altogether on the fundamental social policies that provide benefits and services all Americans should be entitled to, regardless of their residential locations.

INCREASING THE PROGRESSIVITY
OF SALES AND EXCISE TAXES

Most states make use of sales taxes, but not all of them are as punishing to the poor as the southern states. Some achieve a more equitable solution by exempting basic necessities like food for home consumption. We should mount a national campaign to follow suit in the southern states and any other region of the country where basic foodstuffs are taxed, and we should continue with an initiative designed to eliminate sales taxes on medicine and clothing.

Another means to redress regressivity is to follow the lead of states that rebate sales taxes on a means-tested basis, tilting heavily toward low-income families, or refund money through EITCs. At a minimum, one could use the annual consumer expenditure survey to calculate the amount the Jones family would need to pay for a healthy diet and rebate at least that much to households that are currently paying into the system.

Because it is refundable, the federal EITC is by far the most effective way to put much-needed dollars into the hands of working poor families. Twenty-four states have recognized the wisdom of the EITC and enacted statutes of their own, but they are not all created equal. Some states are more generous than others; they send families checks because the liability falls below zero. Encouraging (and even rewarding) the other twenty-six states to enact their own EITCs could provide a boon, particularly in the southern states. Spreading child tax credits and making them refundable as well would have similar positive consequences.

All of these moves would result in taking away revenue that currently flows into state coffers, a prospect that is not enticing in a period of high deficits. But we should not be trying to hold that line on the backs of the poor, not only because it is unfair, but because it is producing social problems that are costly in the present and tend to encourage intergenerational poverty. Moreover, our analysis suggests that at least some of that drain would be stemmed by reducing the need for outlays connected to incarceration, out-of-wedlock births, and early mortality. It would take some time before these changes would translate into additional dollars flowing into tax payments from citizens at work rather than in jail, but as James Heckman's work on the returns from early childhood education makes clear, the wait is worth it because the benefit is notable.[7] We know where the opposite trend is taking the southern states; it isn't a healthy direction.

Still, making tax systems more progressive will not solve the central problem facing the South since the end of Radical Reconstruction. There is too much need and there are too few resources. A more progressive taxation scheme may be able to generate slightly more revenue—and will ensure that the poor are able to hold onto more of their earnings—but it will not be enough to fund social programs and education on a par with the rest of the country without significant federal intervention.[8]

RETHINKING FEDERALISM

As long as major social policies remain in the hands of the states, we are likely to see the interregional inequality detailed in this book persist. This is only partly because the states that are least generous are also the most conservative. The current system requires the poorest states to provide for the poorest citizens by generating revenue for programs like Temporary Assistance for Needy Families (TANF) and Medicaid from the weakest tax base. What are the prospects for shifting some of the power to set eligibility and benefit levels federally?

America's federal structure has resulted in fifty distinct welfare states—each with the responsibility of providing for its poorest citizens. Wealthier states, blessed with either a deeper tax base or fewer needy citizens or both, can afford to provide much more than states burdened with the double whammy of poor citizens and, consequently, a shallow tax base. American social policy in the twentieth century is a largely federal story, with Washington playing an increasingly central—and equalizing—role in the financing of education, welfare, and health care. But, as students of welfare reform can attest, states continue to play a central role.

We think that needs to change. Specifically, we believe that the major safety net programs—particularly TANF and Medicaid—should be regulated and financed at the federal level, just like food stamps, Supplemental Security Income, Medicare, and Social Security. We can follow the National Research Council's recommendations, included in a report on changing the way we calculate the national poverty line, and adjust payments to take into account regional differences in the cost of living.[9] But the basic principle, that all American families are entitled to safety nets of equivalent value, should be made real by taking states out of the equation. The long histories of Social Security and the GI Bill, to name two major social policies that have had durable effects on mobility and economic stability for millions of American families, tell us why this is so important. It took decades to redress the racial inequalities that emerged in the administration of these critical programs because they were left in the hands of the states (a requirement southern senators insisted on in exchange for not torpedoing the central provisions of the New Deal). Leaving these decisions in the hands of states and localities introduces inequalities that punish the poor if they happen to live in states that are content to let them remain destitute.

Does this mean that all poor people would be better off? Not necessarily. Political conflict over how much we want to be our brothers' keepers will remain. Conservatives will continue to argue that market discipline is essential, that welfare corrupts the work ethic, and that taxes are inherently evil. But the debate would be out in the open, and whatever comes of it would be imposed universally. The country would be better off with a national debate over the size and strength of the safety net than a state-driven one.

Toward that end, we should consider resurrecting the Advisory Commission on Intergovernmental Relations. The commission was established by Congress in 1959 with an explicit mandate "to strengthen the American federal system and improve the ability of federal, state, and local governments to work together cooperatively, efficiently, and effectively." For nearly four decades, the commission, comprised of current and former public officials from all levels of government, analyzed everything from the impact of unfunded federal mandates on states to more systematic questions of which level of government should pick up the tab for education or public assistance. The commission was disbanded in 1996—ironically, the same year Congress passed one of the most complex, and controversial, federal-state partnerships: TANF.

BRINGING THE REGIONS
(AND THEIR TAXES) BACK IN

The study of poverty has been one of the most important domains within the general theory of stratification and more recent work that examines the growth in inequality across the United States since the mid-1970s. Yet two critical issues have played almost no role in this powerful literature: regions and taxes. This volume has tried to pull both back into the picture and in doing so has made the case that regressive taxation has contributed to negative outcomes for the poor. It is a policy direction that has always been appealing to the southern states—their populist politicians notwithstanding—and has helped to depress the life chances of poor families in that region to well below what they would have faced in other regions. The extension of this habit to the West—the region of the country with the largest immigrant population—does not augur well for its future. To be sure, we could do better in all parts of the country. Compared to social democracies of western Europe, the whole of the United States looks bad on this score, and our lower levels of life expectancy (and happiness) testify to the distance we have yet to travel as a nation.

But we need to start within our own borders and move to make good on the idea that every American is entitled to the same kind of safety net and the same kind of investment in basic well-being, and that state of residence should not play such a powerful role in determining life chances.

How Many Lags of *x*?

SCOTT M. LYNCH

A common question that arises in social science research involving longitudinal data, that is, panel data in which multiple units are measured at multiple times, is: How long should a predictor variable (*x*) be lagged with respect to the outcome variable (*y*) in a model? Implicitly, the question is: If we incorporate the wrong lag of *x* in our model, how will our results be affected?

In this book, our key *x* variable was the annual state tax burden, and our outcomes included a number of variables reflecting the health, socioeconomic status, and general quality of life within states. Some outcomes, like the out-of-wedlock pregnancy rate, may reasonably be argued to be almost immediately affected by changes in the state tax burden. An increase in the tax burden reduces purchasing power and may lead immediately to reduced contraceptive use, leading to higher rates of teen pregnancy within a few months. In contrast, an outcome like obesity-related mortality may take years to be affected. In such a case, reduced purchasing power may lead to purchasing less healthy foods, which, over time, may increase the risks of mortality.

Given the differences in the length of time it may take for the state tax burden to affect outcomes, it may seem like choosing the right length of time at which to lag *x* would be important and would vary by outcome. Yet there is often very little theory to guide this choice. How many years does it take before a change in the tax burden affects obesity rates? How many years does it take before a change in the tax burden affects high school graduation rates? Is there a single answer to these questions? For example, an immediate increase in tax burden may have both immediate and long-term effects.

Throughout this book, we have chosen to use current values of the tax burden to predict current outcomes, and we have chosen not to include multiple lags of x in our models (a "distributed lag model").[1] One reason that we have chosen not to lag x for long periods is that increasing the number of lags reduces the usable data, because y must be preceded by L observed periods of x; therefore, earlier values of y must be discarded. A reason that we have chosen not to include multiple lags of x is that x-values tend to be highly collinear across time.

SIMULATION STUDY DESIGN

Model Used in Simulation

In this appendix, we conduct a simulation study to examine whether using contemporaneously measured x-values is a reasonable strategy. For generating the data for our simulation, we assume the following two-equation model:

$$x_{it} = \gamma_i + \delta_i t + \sum_{p=1}^{P} \rho_{xp} x_{i(t-p)} + u_{it} \tag{1}$$

$$y_{it} = \alpha_i + \beta_i t + \sum_{q=1}^{Q} \rho_{yq} y_{i(t-q)} + \sum_{s=0}^{S} \phi_s x_{i(t-s)} + e_{it}, \tag{2}$$

where:

x_{it} is the level of the predictor for state i in year t, with $i = 1 \ldots 50$ and $t = 0 \ldots 29$

γ_i is a state-specific baseline level of x, which is assumed to be normally distributed: $\gamma : N(\mu_\gamma, \tau_\gamma)$

δ_i is a state-specific growth rate for x ($\delta : N(\mu_\delta, \tau_\delta)$)

ρ_{xp} is an autoregressive coefficient relating x at lag p to x at time t

u_{it} is an error term that follows the usual regression assumptions,
i.e., $u : N(0,\sigma_u^2)$ and $cov(x,u) = 0$

y_{it} is the level of the outcome for state i in year t

α_i is a state-specific baseline level of y, which is assumed to be
normally distributed: $\alpha : N(\mu_\alpha, \tau_\alpha)$

β_i is a state-specific growth rate for y ($\beta : N(\mu_\beta, \tau_\beta)$)

ρ_{yq} is an autoregressive coefficient relating y at lag q to y at time t

ϕ_s is a "cross-lag" term relating x at time s to y at time t

e_{it} is an error term that follows the usual regression assumptions,
i.e., $e : N(0,\sigma_e^2)$ and $cov(y,e) = 0$ and $cov(x,e) = 0$

This model can be referred to as an "autoregressive latent trajectory" (ALT) model.[2] It combines features of two general models in social science research: the random effects growth model and the autoregressive time series (AR) model.[3]

Equation 1 establishes x as an exogenous process that depends on three components: (1) a state-specific trajectory across time ($\gamma_i + \delta_i t$), (2) the autoregression of x on earlier values of itself ($\Sigma \rho_{xp} x_{i(t-p)}$), and (3) noise ($u_{it}$). Equation 2 establishes y as an endogenous process that depends on lags of x, in addition to the same three types of components described above for x (a state-specific trajectory, an autoregressive process, and noise).

This general two-equation model encapsulates a number of familiar models for longitudinal data. Considering only the equation for x, if the autoregressive portion of equation 1 is eliminated (i.e., $\rho_{xp} = 0$, $\forall p$), the data follow a usual linear growth process. If, instead, the growth component is removed (i.e., $\gamma : N(\mu_y, 0)$ and $\delta : N(0,0)$, x is simply an AR(P) process. Considering equation 2, if y does not depend on x and is not autoregressive (i.e., $\rho_{yq} = 0, \forall q$ and $\phi_s = 0, \forall s$), then y follows a usual latent growth process. If the growth component is removed and y is simply a function of prior values of itself (i.e., $\alpha_i : N(\mu_\alpha, 0), \beta_i = N(0,0)$, and $\phi_s = 0, \forall s$, then y is an AR(Q) process. If the growth parameters are removed, and the AR process is removed, then the data follow a distributed lag process.

The data generation model is a very flexible one and is reasonable for the variables we investigate in the book. Regarding states' tax burdens, the tax rate in any given year varies considerably across states, and the rate of increase (or decrease) in tax rates across time also varies across states. Thus, state tax rates reasonably follow a growth process. In addition, bureaucratic inertia implies that the tax rate in a given year may be highly dependent on the tax rate in previous years, making the tax rate an autoregressive process as well. Finally, there may be year-to-year fluctuations in tax rates that reflect a combination of unobserved factors (noise), like the expiration of sales tax increases or the adoption of new ones in response to natural disasters or other budgetary considerations.

In terms of the outcome variables investigated in this book, we argue that it is reasonable to think of them as following a growth process that varies across states, as well: state-level outcomes, like graduation rates and mortality rates, generally show trending over time that varies by state. Furthermore, they may be autoregressive because of cultural inertia. In addition, year-to-year fluctuations are almost certain because of a combination of a number of unobserved (or unmodeled) factors—natural disasters, for example. And, as we argue in the book, we may expect these outcomes to be responsive to tax rates.

Simulation Parameters

For our simulation study, we aim to determine whether (and to what extent) the estimate of the effect (ϕ_s) of x (taxes) on y (outcomes) is sensitive to the choice of lag of x included in the estimated model. In order to investigate this question, we simulate 1,000 samples each over a design space that involves 400 different combinations of values of the various model parameters shown in equations 1 and 2. Table I.1 presents the key parameter values selected for our simulation study. Some parameters are allowed to vary in order to determine whether the estimate of the effect of x on y is sensitive to variation in the parameters. Other parameters are held constant across all samples.

First, we assumed that both x and y are AR(1) processes; that is, current values of both variables are a function of only the immedi-

Table I.1

Parameter values used in simulation

Equation	Parameter	Variation?	Value(s)	No. of values
x	γ_i	No	$N(0, .05^2)$	1
	δ_i	No	$N(.015, .01^2)$	1
	γ_{xp}	Yes	.4, .8	2
	P	No	1	1
	u_{it}	No	$N(0, .5^2)$	1
y	α_i	No	$N(0, .1^2)$	1
	β_i	No	$N(.015, .01^2)$	1
	ρ_{yq}	Yes	0, .2, .4, .6, .8	5
	Q	No	1	1
	ϕ_s^*	No	.07	1
	S	Yes	0–9	10
	e_{it}	Yes	$N(0, \sigma^2=.5, 1, 1.5, 2)$	4
			TOTAL VARIATIONS	400

*We set $\phi_s = 0$ except for the "true lag" of x that affects y. We then estimated the models using x lagged from 0 to 9 time periods, and for each combination of values, we simulated 1,000 data sets. Overall, then, the simulation involved estimation of 4 million models over 400,000 data sets.

ately prior values of themselves and not values of themselves at greater lags (i.e., $P = Q = 1$). Second, unlike in a typical distributed lag model, where y at a particular time point may be a function of x at numerous lags, we assumed that y responds to x only at a single, specified lag. We allow that lag to vary from 0 (y is a function of the contemporaneous value of x) to 9 (y is a function of x lagged 9 years). To clarify these constraints, equations 1 and 2 simplify to:

$$x_{it} = \gamma_i + \delta_i t + \rho_x x_{i(t-1)} + u_{it} \tag{3}$$

$$y_{it} = \alpha_i + \beta_i t + \rho_y y_{i(t-1)} + \phi_s x_{i(t-s)} + e_{it}, \tag{4}$$

where s is the lag of x that influences y and s ranges from 0 to 9.

In addition to these constraints, we set the mean and variances of the growth parameters (μ_γ, μ_δ, μ_α, μ_β, and τ_γ, τ_δ, τ_α, τ_β) to be constant across all samples. Finally, we fixed the effect of x (at the appropriate lag) on y (ϕ_s) to a constant value. For these various parameters, altering their values is not expected to have any effect on the overall pattern of the simulation results. For example, changing ϕ_s would affect the model R^2 in a predictable fashion (the mean squared error of the estimates would change), but it should not affect the extent to which the parameter can be estimated correctly (the bias should be the same, regardless of the true value of ϕ_s).

We allowed four parameters to vary in the simulation. First, we allowed the autoregressive parameter for x (ρ_x) to take two values (.4 and .8), making x a weakly rather than strongly autoregressive process. Second, we allowed the autoregressive parameter for y (ρ_y) to take five unique values (0, .2, .4, .6, and .8), meaning y ranges from being nonautoregressive to highly autoregressive (net of other model parameters). Third, we varied the level of noise present in y by allowing the error variance parameter (σ_ϵ^2) to take four distinct values: .5, 1, 1.5, and 2. These values ultimately lead to model R^2-values that range from about 5 percent to about 60 percent. Finally, as stated above, although we did not vary the effect of x on y (ϕ_s), we *did* vary the "true lag" at which x affects y.

Overall, then, the design space consists of $2 \times 5 \times 4 \times 10 = 400$ parameter combinations. We simulated 1,000 samples for each of these combinations, yielding a total of 400,000 samples. We then estimated our models ten ways on each sample, by incorporating x measured at different lags in the model (from including contemporaneously measured x to x at a nine-year lag). Thus, we estimated 4 million models.

For each of the 4,000 sets of models, we saved two measures reflecting the ability of the model to estimate the true value of the ϕ parameter: the mean squared error (MSE) of the estimate and the average bias of the estimate (BIAS) over the 1,000 samples.

While the simulation design model involves the combination of a linear random effects growth model with an autoregressive structure for both predictor and outcome variables, the results presented in this book are from a fixed-effects model that includes fixed effects for states and years. Thus, for each simulated data set, we estimate such a fixed-effects model. Although the usual strategy for a simulation study is to use the same data generation model and estimation/test model, in reality we have no way of knowing the true underlying data generation process. We feel, however, that our data generation model is realistic, and our modeling strategy for the data is an appropriate, and very general, model for this type of data. The fixed-effects approach essentially eliminates the latent intercept of the growth processes for x and y from the data, and although including year fixed effects assumes no between-state variation in growth rates, it does allow nonlinearity in growth, while the random effects data generation model did not.

Figure I.1 consists of four plots demonstrating the simulation and estimation process for *one* of the 4,000 design/estimation combinations. Specifically, σ_e^2 was set to $.5^2$, the true lag of x was 1 (i.e., x affects y at a one-year lag), the autoregressive parameter for x (ρ_x) was .8, the autoregressive parameter for y (ρ_y) was 0, and the model used estimates the effect of contemporaneously measured x on y. In other words, there is a mismatch between the true and estimated lag at which x affects y.

The top left plot in the figure shows simulated state-specific trajectories of the "tax burden" (x) for a single simulated sample. Each state's trajectory is represented with a line. The top right plot shows the corresponding trajectories for a hypothetical outcome. The bottom left plot in the figure shows the estimates for the effect of x on y (ϕ_s) across the 1,000 simulated samples under the aforementioned design. The bottom right plot in the figure shows these estimates in histogram format. In each of the bottom figures, the true value of ϕ_s is represented with a solid line, and the mean of the 1,000 sample estimates is represented with a dashed line. As the plots show, under this design, using the contemporaneous value of x to predict y when the true lag at which x affects y is 1 tends to bias the estimate of ϕ_s downward.

Simulation Results

A number of summaries are possible given the extent of the simulation. Here, we highlight the key findings of the simulation (complete

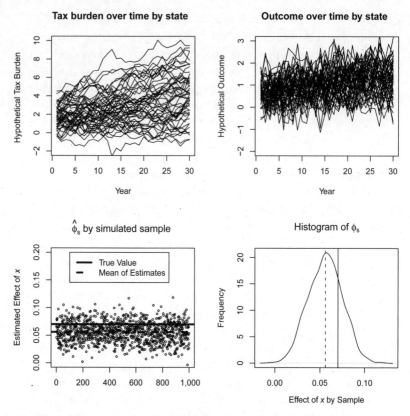

Figure I.1. An example of simulated data for x and y (top half) and estimates of effect of x on y across 1,000 simulated data sets (bottom half). The top left plot shows trajectories of "tax burden" across year by state. The top right plot shows trajectories of outcome across year by state. The bottom left plot shows estimates of the effect of tax burden on the outcome across 1,000 simulated samples when contemporaneous x is included in the model but the true lag is one year. The bottom right plot shows the histogram of these estimates. Both bottom figures show the true value (0.07, solid line) and the mean of the sample estimates (dashed line). The bias is negative.

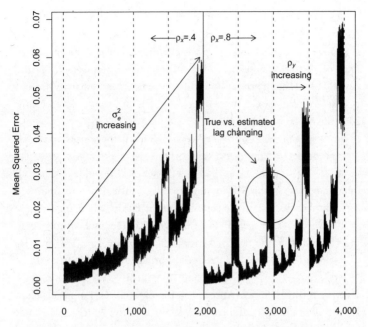

Figure I.2. The mean squared error (MSE) of estimates of the effect of x on y across the 4,000 parameter/estimation combinations in the simulation. Simulated parameter combination (each point summarizes 1,000 samples).

results, as well as the program code used to generate the data and estimate the models, are available from the author of this appendix). An overarching question the simulation can answer is: How well does the state and year fixed-effects model perform, in terms of capturing the true parameter value for the effect of "tax burden" (x) on outcomes (y) (parameter φ_s)? The second question, the key focus of the simulation, is: What happens if the wrong lag of x is included in the model; in particular, what is the consequence of modeling x at lag 0?

Figure I.2 presents the entire simulation results with respect to MSE. Recall that the simulation involved changing $\rho_x, \rho_y, \sigma_e^2$, and the true and estimated lag of x. The figure shows the results of each of these combinations. ρ_x took two values in the simulation: .4 and .8. To the left of the solid vertical line in the figure are the results for the samples in which ρ_x = .4; to the right of the solid vertical line are the results for the samples in which ρ_x = .8.

Within these two halves of the figure (divided by ρ_x), the error variance of y (σ_e^2) increases from left to right across the dashed vertical lines. The dashed vertical lines differentiate σ_e^2 as it changes from .5 to 2 at increments of .5 units (four values). Thus, as σ_e^2 increases, the MSE increases quadratically.

Between each set of the dashed vertical lines, ρ_y increases from 0 to .8 (at increments of .2 units; five values). Observe that to make this explanation concrete, in all cases there is a cluster of MSE values that stands out: when ρ_y = .8, the MSE jumps upward drastically. This finding is especially noticeable in the right half of the figure (where ρ_x = .8).

Finally, between each set of dashed vertical lines and within changing values for ρ_y, the true and estimated lag of x varies. The true lag of x (produced in the data generation process) increases from 0 to 9 "years" from left to right (from contemporaneous with y to a nine-year lag). Within this change in true lag, the dark clusters of points show the result of changing the *estimated* lag of x. In the figure, an example of this combination of 100 true lag versus estimated lag combinations is highlighted with a circle, and we discuss the pattern of this cluster of points below.

Overall, with respect to the general performance of the model used throughout the book, the results suggest that changing σ_e^2 and changing ρ_y produce the greatest changes in MSE. This result is anticipated because increasing the error variance in the outcome (i.e., increasing σ_e^2) adds noise to the outcome, and ρ_y is not modeled with the fixed-effects model used throughout the book. In order to gain a better understanding of the performance of the model, then, the bias in the estimation of the parameter for the effect of x on y should be examined.

Figure I.3 replicates figure I.2 for bias. We do not provide as much detailed annotation in this figure as in figure I.2, but the pattern shown is similar. In figure I.3, we provide a horizontal reference line at 0. Points falling above this line indicate that the model used in the book *over-estimates* the effect of x on y, while points falling below the line indicate that the model *underestimates* the effect of x on y. That is, the model

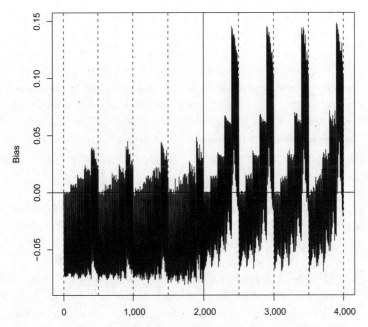

Figure I.3. The bias of estimates of the effect of *x* on *y* across the 4,000 parameter/estimation combinations in the simulation. Simulated parameter combination (each point summarizes 1,000 samples).

provides a *conservative* estimate of the relationship between tax burden and outcomes. Overall, of the 4,000 combinations of data/parameters in the simulation, the effect of tax burden on outcomes is underestimated 2,865 times and overestimated 1,135 times. In other words, based on these simulation results, the model used throughout the book *underestimates* the true relationship between tax burden and outcomes just under 75 percent of the time. Put another way, the results presented in this book are most likely conservative estimates of the effect of tax burden on outcomes.

We now turn to the second question: What is the consequence of using the wrong lag of *x*? While we cannot know the true data generation process that underlies the observed data, we do know that, throughout the book, we have used contemporaneous values of x in predicting y. The pattern of the consequence of using the true versus estimated lag of x in predicting y is constant across the entire simulation. When we use the value of x that is contemporaneous with y (i.e., lag of x is 0), the average bias is $-.0326$. That is, our estimated effect of x is 54 percent of the true effect (we underestimate the effect by 47 percent). In sum, then, it seems that using the contemporaneous value of x, on average, leads to conservative results.

REFERENCES

1. C. W. Ostrom, *Time Series Analysis: Regression Techniques*, Sage University Paper Series on Quantitative Applications in the Social Sciences, no. 07–009, 2nd ed. (Thousand Oaks, CA: 1990).

2. K. A. Bollen and P. J. Curran, "Autoregressive Latent Trajectory (ALT) Models: A Synthesis of Two Traditions," *Sociological Methods and Research* 32:3 (2004): 336–83.

3. J. D. Hamilton, *Time Series Analysis* (Princeton: Princeton University Press, 1994) and Ostrom, *Time Series Analysis: Regression Techniques*.

Tables

Table II.1

Infant mortality rates (per 1,000) by race, 2004–2006

	White	Black	Hispanic
Alabama	6.98	13.76	7.43
Alaska	5.01	NA	NA
Arizona	6.05	12.3	6.72
Arkansas	6.96	13.99	6.28
California	4.67	11.4	4.91
Colorado	5.18	13.97	7.01
Connecticut	3.97	13.38	7.76
Delaware	6.31	15.02	5.54
District of Columbia	3.22	18.46	NA
Florida	5.86	12.76	5.07
Georgia	6.07	12.95	5.15
Hawaii	3.66	20.85	6.11
Idaho	5.97	NA	7.32
Illinois	5.88	14.39	6.21
Indiana	6.99	16.07	6.74

(continued)

Table II.1 (continued)

	White	Black	Hispanic
Iowa	4.96	8.18	5.01
Kentucky	6.48	12.54	7.35
Louisiana	7	14.69	5.65
Maine	6.16	NA	NA
Maryland	5.55	12.94	5.26
Massachusetts	3.99	10.31	6.38
Michigan	5.74	15.66	7.32
Minnesota	4.36	9.62	4.27
Mississippi	6.8	15.4	5.74
Missouri	6.45	13.79	6.23
Montana	5.03	NA	NA
Nebraska	5.25	12.15	5.84
Nevada	5.53	14.33	5.1
New Hampshire	5.33	NA	NA
New Jersey	3.68	11.76	5.14
New Mexico	6.75	NA	5.41
New York	4.61	11.46	5.29
North Carolina	6.37	15.66	6.17
North Dakota	5.37	NA	NA
Ohio	6.35	15.92	5.61
Oklahoma	7.68	13.07	5.38
Oregon	5.54	9.42	5.37
Pennsylvania	5.84	13.82	7.71
Rhode Island	3.97	11.42	7.95
South Carolina	6.28	14.34	7.37
South Dakota	6.2	NA	NA
Tennessee	6.87	15.87	6.5
Texas	5.83	12.11	5.54
Utah	4.74	NA	5.31
Vermont	5.64	NA	NA
Virginia	5.69	13.79	5.28

	White	Black	Hispanic
Washington	4.49	8.12	4.82
West Virginia	7.33	15.09	NA
Wisconsin	5.01	16.94	5.73
Wyoming	7.33	NA	NA
United States	5.7	13.5	5.5

SOURCE: Kaiser Family Foundation, State Health Facts, http://www
.statehealthfacts.org/comparetable.jsp?cat=2&ind=48, accessed
September 3, 2010.

Table II.2

Deaths due to heart disease
(per 100,000) by race, 2006

	White	Black	Other
Alabama	256.5	300.6	91.6
Alaska	164.1	NA	162.6
Arizona	179.4	204.7	129.6
Arkansas	234.4	310.2	78
California	203.7	293.7	116.2
Colorado	163	204.5	81.7
Connecticut	181.6	201.1	96.1
Delaware	218.9	274.1	158.2
District of Columbia	145	312.5	156.1
Florida	184.5	238.1	80.8
Georgia	218.1	257.3	97.1
Hawaii	166.3	NA	156.7
Idaho	179.7	NA	131.3
Illinois	207.9	296.6	101.5
Indiana	221.9	251.8	118
Iowa	193.5	226.6	NA

(continued)

Table II.2 (continued)

	White	Black	Other
Kansas	186.8	252.9	167.5
Kentucky	250.5	277.9	89.1
Louisiana	241.4	284.9	105.6
Maine	185.5	NA	NA
Maryland	207.4	259.8	88.6
Massachusetts	177.9	188.7	67.5
Michigan	228.1	333.1	130.9
Minnesota	143.8	125.9	92.8
Mississippi	274.8	341.2	122.8
Missouri	227	293	86.1
Montana	168	NA	210.7
Nebraska	174.1	213.1	192.1
Nevada	243.3	272.4	143.4
New Hampshire	186.4	NA	NA
New Jersey	214.7	247.6	99.6
New Mexico	183	196.1	137.6
New York	243.4	269.9	127.1
North Carolina	199.7	244.2	157.1
North Dakota	178.1	NA	199.5
Ohio	224.2	275.7	71.5
Oklahoma	260.5	329.2	210.4
Oregon	169.8	182.9	92.7
Pennsylvania	221.9	272	77.9
Rhode Island	224.2	243.4	128.1
South Carolina	204.8	256.8	84.8
South Dakota	177.7	NA	285.3
Tennessee	237.6	306.6	99.6
Texas	207.8	279.7	84.7
Utah	160.5	204.6	101.9
Vermont	178.2	NA	NA
Virginia	193.4	240.5	90.5
Washington	179.6	209.9	111.9

Table II.2 (continued)

	White	Black	Other
West Virginia	249.6	251.9	NA
Wisconsin	187.6	250.7	171.4
Wyoming	187.3	NA	NA
United States	207.7	271.3	117.8

SOURCE: Kaiser Family Foundation, State Health Facts, http://www
.statehealthfacts.org/comparetable.jsp?ind=79&cat=2, accessed
September 3, 2010.

Table II.3

Deaths due to stroke or cerebrovascular disease
(per 100,000) by race, 2006

	White	Black
Alabama	55.3	83.6
Alaska	47.1	NA
Arizona	38.3	53
Arkansas	54.7	91.7
California	47.3	67.4
Colorado	41.9	56.7
Connecticut	35.8	51.3
Delaware	40.1	61.7
District of Columbia	27.3	45.8
Florida	35.1	71.2
Georgia	48.5	69.3
Hawaii	35.9	NA
Idaho	52.8	NA
Illinois	45.7	67.9
Indiana	49.1	75.9
Iowa	48.4	NA
Kansas	48.1	75.2
Kentucky	50	69
Louisiana	49	79.7
Maine	43.6	NA

(continued)

Table II.3 (continued)

	White	Black
Maryland	44	55.1
Massachusetts	38.9	46.1
Michigan	46.3	64.1
Minnesota	42.1	46.1
Mississippi	49.3	71.2
Missouri	49.8	69.7
Montana	47.1	NA
Nebraska	46.6	57.5
Nevada	44.5	66.3
New Hampshire	36.8	NA
New Jersey	35.8	58.7
New Mexico	39.1	NA
New York	31.3	31.3
North Carolina	52.8	78.3
North Dakota	42.1	NA
Ohio	48.2	60.3
Oklahoma	57.6	71.9
Oregon	56.2	84.9
Pennsylvania	45.3	67
Rhode Island	39	NA
South Carolina	51.9	77
South Dakota	51.1	NA
Tennessee	58.3	79
Texas	48.1	73.1
Utah	44.3	NA
Vermont	37.6	NA
Virginia	48.4	73.8
Washington	47.1	46.1
West Virginia	51.8	62.7
Wisconsin	46.6	55.5
United States	44.7	65.2

SOURCE: Kaiser Family Foundation, State Health Facts, http://www
.statehealthfacts.org/comparetable.jsp?ind=124&cat=2, accessed
September 3, 2010.

Table II.4

Simulating the impact of different tax structures

	Coefficient from fixed-effects model	Difference of South and average tax	Additional change on outcome (per 100,000)
High school completion (1982–2002)			
All non-South	-0.003	$169.51	+0.438
Northeast		$276.49	+0.715
Unmarried Births (1990–2006)			
All non-South	0.0007	$281.35	-0.185
Northeast		$476.85	-0.314
Percent employed (1982–2006)			
All non-South	-0.0006	$210.66	+0.131
Northeast		$354.89	+0.221

NOTES

PREFACE

1. See Tax Foundation, *State Sales, Gasoline, Cigarette, and Alcohol Tax Rates by State, 2000–2010* (Washington, DC), http://www.taxfoundation .org/taxdata/show/245.html, accessed September 3, 2010.

2. Only 24 percent of the nation's private and 12 percent of its public four-year university graduates have loans of this size. See Sandy Baum and Patricia Steele, *Who Borrows Most? Bachelor's Degree Recipients with High Levels of Student Debt* (College Board, 2010), http://advocacy .collegeboard.org/sites/default/files/Trends-Who-Borrows-Most-Brief .pdf, accessed May 18, 2010.

3. Only 4 percent of those graduating from for-profit colleges leave debt free, compared with 28 percent of graduates from private universities and 38 percent from public universities (ibid.).

4. Only debtors who can prove that repayment would cause "undue hardship" can get rid of education loans of this kind, and it is very hard to qualify, even for someone like Bea, because Congress has never defined what the term *undue hardship* actually means.

5. FinAid, *Low Odds of a Successful Undue Hardship Discharge* (Mark Kantrowitz, Publisher), http://www.finaid.org/questions/bankruptcy .phtml, accessed May 18, 2010.

6. These benefits will disappear as a source of household income when the children reach eighteen.

7. For the distribution of poverty in the United States by region over time, see U.S. Census Bureau, *Distribution of the Poor by Region,* Table 17, Historical Poverty Tables (Washington, DC), http://www.census.gov/hhes/www/poverty/data/historical/people.html, accessed September 3, 2010. The distribution of poor households has been remarkably stable over the past four decades. For the number of poor children by region, see National Center for Children in Poverty, 50-State Demographics Wizard (child poverty data compiled using microdata from the U.S. Census Bureau's Current Population Survey) (Washington, DC), http://www.nccp.org/tools/demographics, accessed May 24, 2010. We excluded Delaware, Maryland, and the District of Columbia in our definition of southern states.

8. Although all of the other names of interviewees in this book are real and their identities accurately described, this individual requested anonymity. Hence we have changed the name of the town where she lives and other identifying details.

9. See Isaac William Martin, Ajay K. Mehrotra, and Monica Prasad, "The Thunder of History: The Origins and Development of the New Fiscal Sociology," in *The New Fiscal Sociology: Taxation in Comparative and Historical Perspective,* ed. Isaac William Martin, Ajay K. Mehrotra, and Monica Prasad (Cambridge: Cambridge University Press, 2009).

10. See especially Kimberly Morgan and Monica Prasad, "The Origins of Tax Systems: A French-American Comparison," *American Journal of Sociology* 114:5 (2009): 1350–94.

11. For example, I. W. Martin, *The Permanent Tax Revolt: How the Property Tax Transformed American Politics* (Palo Alto, CA: Stanford University Press, 2008).

12. Barry Bluestone and Bennett Harrison, *The Deindustrialization of America* (New York: Basic Books, 1984).

ONE. THE EVOLUTION OF SOUTHERN TAX STRUCTURES

1. Kimberly J. Morgan and Monica Prasad, "The Origins of Tax Systems: A French-American Comparison," *American Journal of Sociology* 114:5 (2009): 1350–94.

2. Robin L. Einhorn, *American Taxation, American Slavery* (Chicago: University of Chicago Press, 2006), p. 228.

3. Robin L. Einhorn, "Species of Property: The American Property-Tax Uniformity Clauses Reconsidered," *Journal of Economic History* 61:4 (2001).

4. Einhorn, *American Taxation,* p. 209.

5. As Einhorn explains, uniformity clauses specified that "no one species of property from which a tax may be collected shall be taxed any higher than any other species of property of equal value" (ibid.).

6. In "Species of Property" Einhorn argues convincingly that as of 1818 Illinois should be added to this list because of the large presence of slaves in what was formally a "free" state.

7. See "The History of Taxation," published by the Tax History Project, http://www.taxanalysts.com/museum/1861-1865.htm, accessed May 24, 2010.

8. Rose Razaghian, "Financing the Civil War: The Confederacy's Financial Strategy," Yale International Center for Finance Working Paper 04–45 (2005), p. 1.

9. Ibid., p. 15.

10. Ibid., p. 31.

11. Ibid., p. 21.

12. Elna C. Green, ed., *Before the New Deal: Social Welfare in the South, 1830–1930* (Athens: University of Georgia Press, 1999), p. xiv.

13. Ibid., p. xv. Green cites P. Wallenstein, *From Slave South to New South: Public Policy in Nineteenth-Century Georgia* (Chapel Hill: University of North Carolina Press, 1987), p. 131–39.

14. Ibid.

15. Ibid.

16. J. Mills Thornton III, "Fiscal Policy and the Failure of Radical Reconstruction in the Lower South," in *Region, Race and Reconstruction: Essays in Honor of C. Vann Woodward,* ed. J. Morgan Kousser and James M. McPherson, 349–94 (New York: Oxford University Press, 1982), p. 368.

17. Ibid.

18. C. V. Woodward, *Origins of the New South, 1877–1913* (Baton Rouge: Louisiana State University Press, 1971), p. 59.

19. April 26, 1890; cited in Woodward, p. 59.

20. Woodward, p. 61–62.

21. Eric Foner, *Forever Free: The Story of Emancipation and Reconstruction* (New York: Knopf, 2005), p. 204.

22. Eric Foner, *Nothing but Freedom: Emancipation and Its Legacy* (Baton Rouge: Louisiana State University Press, 1983), p. 70.

23. J. Morgan Kousser, "Progressivism—For Middle-Class Whites Only: North Carolina Education, 1880–1910," *Journal of Southern Economic History* 46:2 (1980): 169–95.

24. Ibid., p. 185.

25. Yet the drive among poor blacks and whites for better education catalyzed during Radical Reconstruction persisted. Limited by a regressive tax structure that prevented the redistribution of funds from wealthier to poorer areas, Kousser finds, in North Carolina "school taxes were higher in poor than relatively rich counties, and much higher among blacks than whites" (ibid., p. 191).

26. Einhorn, "Species of Property," p. 248.

27. Claudia Goldin and Lawrence Katz, *The Race between Education and Technology* (Cambridge: Harvard University Press, 2008).

28. Ibid., p. 156–57.

29. Ibid., p. 197.

30. During this period the use of the general property tax to fund government was under fire because of its inequity and inefficiency, especially in the North where tax rates were high. See Edwin R. A. Seligman, "The General Property Tax," *Political Science Quarterly* 5:1 (1890): 24–64. Loathing of the property tax contributed to the movement for a federal income tax by citizens who hoped those revenues could be used to ease the high taxes levied by state and local governments. See Kimberly J. Morgan and Monica Prasad, "The Origins of Tax Systems: A French-American Comparison," *American Journal of Sociology* 114:5 (2009): 1350–94. Also see Alan Furman Westin, "The Populist Movement and the Campaign of 1896," *Journal of Politics* 15:1 (1953): 3–41.

31. Timothy Egan, *The Worst Hard Time: The Untold Story of Those Who Survived the Great American Dust Bowl* (New York: Mariner Books, 2006).

32. Lizabeth Cohen, *Making a New Deal: Industrial Workers in Chicago 1919–1939* (Cambridge: Cambridge University Press, 1991).

33. Roger Biles, *The South and the New Deal* (Lexington: University of Kentucky Press, 1994), p. 58.

34. Gavin Wright, "The New Deal and the Modernization of the South," *Federal History Journal* 2 (2010): 58–73.

35. Biles, p. 23–24.

36. Ibid., p. 23.

37. Ibid., p. 24.

38. Ibid.

39. Ibid., p. 25.

40. Ibid., p. 64.

41. Ibid., p. 28–32.

42. During the early 1930s, a group of Columbia University professors conducted a study on the debates over sales tax legislation in a number of states, based on letters, news dispatches, and interviews with state officials, businessmen, and other interested parties. See R. Haig and C. Shoup, *The Sales Taxes in the American States* (New York: Columbia University Press, 1934).

43. *The Atlanta Constitution,* February 3, 1934.

44. Haig and Shoup, p. 200.

45. A central motivating force in North Carolina for enacting sales taxes was the $15 million in debt that the state had accumulated, in large part to finance education. The state provided almost all school operating costs, with little support from local property taxes. See Haig and Shoup.

46. Haig and Shoup, p. 186–87.

47. "Exemptions Fail to End Tax Fight; Early Vote Seen," *Washington Post,* March 22, 1932.

48. "The Proposed Sales Tax," *New Journal and Guide,* December 9, 1933.

49. Carl Shoup and Louis Haimoff, "The Sales Tax," *Columbia Law Review* 34:5 (1934): 809–30. See p. 812.

50. As of 1955, a number of states, including California, Connecticut, Maryland, and Maine, had excluded food for home consumption from the sales tax. See J. F. Due, "The Nature and Structure of Sales Taxation," *Vanderbilt Law Review* 9 (1955): 123.

For dates on food exemptions since 1975, see C. A. Agostini, *The Effect of Sales Tax Rates on Food Exemptions,* Social Science Research Network Working Paper, 2004, http://papers.ssrn.com/sol3/papers.cfm?abstract _id=964929, accessed May 24, 2010.

51. Corporate and individual income taxes were also enacted in the gilded age of the 1920s and 1930s, but owing to the comparatively weaker development of industry in the South and the lower income structure of its people, these taxes generated less revenue there than they did in the eastern, western, and midwestern states. For dates of adoption of major taxes by state, see Advisory Commission on Intergovernmental Relations, *Significant Features of Fiscal Federalism,* vol. 1. (Washington, DC: U.S. Government Printing Office, 1994).

52. See Katherine Newman and Elisabeth Jacobs, *Brothers' Keepers? The Limits of Solidarity from the New Deal to the Second Gilded Age* (Princeton: Princeton University Press, 2010).

53. Ira Katznelson, *When Affirmative Action Was White* (New York: Norton, 2005).

54. Lee J. Alson and Joseph P Ferrie, *Southern Paternalism and the American Welfare State: Economics, Politics, and Institutions in the South, 1865–1965* (Cambridge: Cambridge University Press, 1999), p. 70.

55. Ibid., p. 69.

56. Ibid., p. 71.

57. "Table 7–13. Maximum AFDC/TANF Benefit for a Family of Three (Parent with Two Children) July 1970–January 2003," in *The Green Book* (Washington, DC: U.S. House of Representatives, Committee on Ways and Means, 2003), http://waysandmeans.house.gov/media/ pdf/greenbook2003/Section7.pdf, accessed May 24, 2010.

58. As Lizbeth Cohen details in *A Consumer's Republic,* high property taxes do not always translate into a well-funded public sector. In

the two decades immediately following WWII, New Jersey was one of three states that lacked both an income and a sales tax; the state therefore posted the lowest *statewide* revenue generated per capita in the country. The public sector functioned mostly on revenue generated from the nation's highest property tax, which was raised and spent at the local level, yielding tremendous inequality in public sector spending between localities, particularly in education. See Lizbeth Cohen, *A Consumer's Republic* (New York: Knopf, 2003), p. 231–34.

59. Gavin Wright, *Old South, New South: Revolutions in the Southern Economy since the Civil War* (New York: Basic Books, 1986).

60. As Wright (ibid., p. 260) details, economic growth in the South was further buttressed by federal investments, notably military installations.

61. U.S. Census Bureau, *Poverty, by Region,* Table 9, Historical Poverty Tables (Washington, DC), http://www.census.gov/hhes/www/poverty/data/historical/people.html, accessed May 24, 2010.

TWO. BARRIERS TO CHANGE

1. State of Arkansas, Bureau of Legislative Research, *A Summary of Legislative Supermajority Requirements,* Report #05–101 (2005), http://staging.arkleg.state.ar.us/Policy/docs/Project%2005-101.pdf, accessed May 24, 2010.

2. The state sales tax rate is 6.0 percent, but an additional tax of up to 5.5 percent in some jurisdictions brings the total to as much as 11.5 percent. See Tax Foundation, *Comparison of State and Local Retail Sales Taxes, 2010* (Washington, DC: 2010), http://www.taxpolicycenter.org/taxfacts/Content/PDF/state_local_sales_tax.pdf, accessed May 24, 2010.

3. Bert Waisanen, *State Tax and Expenditure Limits, 2008* (Washington, DC: National Conference of State Legislatures), http://www.ncsl.org/IssuesResearch/BudgetTax/StateTaxandExpenditureLimits2008/tabid/12633/Default.aspx, accessed May 24, 2010.

4. Brian Knight, "Supermajority Voting Requirements for Tax Increases: Evidence from the States," *Journal of Public Economics* 76 (2000): 41–67.

5. Center for Fiscal Responsibility, *States with a Supermajority Requirement to Raise Taxes* (Washington, DC), http://www.fiscalaccountability.org/index.php?content = supersub1, accessed May 24, 2010.

6. Daniel Mullins and Bruce Wallin, "Tax and Expenditure Limitations: Introduction and Overview," *Public Budgeting and Finance* (Winter 2004): 2–15.

7. Bruce P. Ely and Howard P. Walthall, "State Constitutional Limitations on Taxing and Spending: A Comparison of the Alabama Constitution of 1901 to Its Counterparts," *Cumberland Law Review* 33 (2002): 463.

8. See knightsims.com, accessed May 24, 2010. The Web site is maintained by plaintiffs in *Knight-Sims v. Alabama*. The contact is Birmingham, AL, Attorney James U. Blacksher, counsel for the plaintiffs.

9. Rebecca Walker, "After 26 Years, *Knight-Sims vs. Alabama* Case Settled at Last," *Flora-Ala Student Newspaper*, February 22, 2007, http://media.www.florala.net/media/storage/paper293/news/2007/02/22/News/After.26.Years.KnightsSims.V.Alabama.Case.Settled.At.Last-2745817-page2.shtml and www.knightsims.com, accessed May 24, 2010.

10. What follows is a summary of the historical background compiled by the plaintiffs, relying in part on the expert testimony and submitted affidavits of Alabama historians Dr. J. Mills Thornton, Dr. Robert J. Norrell, and Dr. Henry J. McKiven.

11. *Knight-Sims v. Alabama* Plaintiffs' Post-Trial Proposed Findings of Fact and Conclusions of Law Regarding Vestiges of Segregation in Alabama's Property Tax System. Filed in the U.S. District Court for the Northern District of Alabama, Southern Division, paragraph 60.

12. Wayne Flint, *Alabama in the Twentieth Century* (Tuscaloosa: University of Alabama Press, 2004), p. 17.

13. According to the plaintiffs in *Knight-Sims v. Alabama* (*Knight-Sims v. Alabama* Plaintiffs' Post-Trial Proposed Findings of Fact, paragraph 96), "the following sections in the 1901 Alabama Constitution are traceable to the State's *de jure* system of racial segregation and discrimination against black citizens with respect to the revenues and funds required to provide them equal access to public education:

"Ala. Const. § 214, as amended, which limits the millage rate of ad valorem taxation the Alabama Legislature may place on taxable property;

"Ala. Const. § 215, as amended, which limits the millage rate of ad valorem taxation counties may place on taxable property;

"Ala. Const. § 216, as amended, which limits the millage rate of ad valorem taxation municipalities may place on taxable property;

"Ala. Const. § 269, as amended, which limits the millage rate of ad valorem taxation counties may place on taxable property for the benefit of public education, and which further requires approval of these property taxes by the voters of the county in a referendum election."

14. Ibid., paragraph 101.

15. Ibid., paragraph 119.

16. As the plaintiff's historical background notes, "Black Belt and urban industrial interests successfully used the argument that it is unfair for white property owners to pay for the education of blacks to produce all the state constitutional barriers to property taxes from 1875 to the present, including the 1971 and 1978 Lid Bill amendments" (ibid., paragraph 183).

17. Ibid., paragraph 191. See Susan Pace Hamill, *An Argument for Tax Reform Based on Judeo-Christian Ethics,* 54 Ala. L. Rev. 1 (2002).

18. See Susan Pace Hamill, *An Argument for Tax Reform Based on Judeo-Christian Ethics* and Susan Pace Hamill, *Constitutional Reform in Alabama: A Necessary Step Toward Achieving a Fair and Efficient Tax Structure,* 33 Cumb. L. Rev. 437 (2002–03).

19. B. G. Knight, "Supermajority Voting Requirements for Tax Increases: Evidence from the States," *Journal of Public Economics* 76:1 (2000): 41–67.

20. John Charles Bradbury and Joseph M. Johnson, "Do Supermajority Rules Limit or Enhance Majority Tyranny? Evidence from the US States, 1960–1997," *Public Choice* 127 (2006): 437–49.

21. D. R. Mullins and B. A. Wallin, "Tax and Expenditure Limitations: Introduction and Overview," *Public Budgeting & Finance* 24 (2004): 2–15, p. 5.

22. Isaac Martin, *The Permanent Tax Revolt: How Property Tax Transformed American Politics* (Stanford: Stanford University Press, 2008), p. 52.

23. Ibid., p. 75.

24. See A. Alesina and E. L. Glaeser, *Fighting Poverty in the US and Europe: A World of Difference* (New York: Oxford University Press, 2005).

25. Isaac Martin, personal communication, April 2010.

26. Timothy Conlan, *From New Federalism to Devolution: Twenty-five Years of Intergovernmental Reform* (Washington, DC: Brookings Institution Press, 1998).

27. Ibid., p. 5–6.

28. Ibid., p. 295.

29. Max Sawicky, "The New American Devolution: Problems and Prospects," in *The End of Welfare? Consequences of Federal Devolution for the Nation,* ed. Max Sawicky, p. 3–24 (Armonk, NY: M.E. Sharpe, 1999).

30. Elizabeth Kolbert, "The 1992 Campaign: The Governor: Clinton in Arkansas—A Special Report: An Early Loss Cast Clinton as a Leader by Consensus," *New York Times,* September 28, 1992.

31. Peter Applebome, "Clinton Record in Leading Arkansas: Successes, but Not Without Criticism," *New York Times,* December 22, 1991.

32. "Arkansas Overhauling Its Education Program," *New York Times,* November 20, 1983.

33. Ibid.

34. *Arkansas Democrat-Gazette,* January 27, 1991, Editorial.

35. The experience of Governor Ray Mabus of Mississippi, a contemporary of Clinton's, was similar. Mabus was elected in 1987 at the age of 39. Constitutional reform was his signature issue, but his proposal was defeated in 1988. Even black legislators voted against it out of concern that a convention might reverse the victories blacks had achieved. Mabus proposed to increase the average annual salary of the state's teachers by $3,800 and provide funding for state agency, community college, and university facilities. His education reform initiative—BEST (Better Education for Success Tomorrow)—was approved by the legislature in 1990, but funding for the program fell through because Mabus refused to increase sales or income taxes to fund the program and the legislature would not approve use of a lottery to fund the program. He lost reelection in 1991. Subsequently, the Mississippi sales tax was raised from 6 to 7 percent (in 1992).

36. Based on findings of "a personal interview research survey conducted among 2,195 men and women 18 years or over living in pri-

vate households in the continental United States ... during the period March 15 through April 8, 1972." Advisory Commission on Intergovernmental Relations, *Public Opinion and Taxes* (Washington, DC: May 1972), http://www.library.unt.edu/gpo/acir/Reports/survey/S-1.pdf, accessed September 3, 2010.

37. The regional differences are instructive. Northeastern respondents were more enamored of federal income tax (43 percent) than were those in any other part of the country, and the southern respondents had the least affection for it (29 percent). Northeasterners were not nearly as comfortable with the state sales tax (23 percent) as the respondents in all the other parts of the country, including the South, where 37 percent thought it was the fairest way to raise revenue. Indeed, these data suggest that it was the Northeast that was an outlier in rejecting regressive taxation, while the South, the West, and the north central states were fairly uniform in embracing sales taxes. When asked what vehicle their state government should turn to if it needed to raise revenue, the first choice of southern respondents was the sales tax, to the tune of 43 percent, but western respondents were even more insistent this was the way to go. Some 54 percent of them pointed to the sales tax as the best way to raise new funds. Northeastern residents were less enthusiastic: 38 percent recommended the state sales tax (ibid.).

38. See chapter 5 for data discussion on the composition of regional tax revenues.

39. C. Cornwell, D. B. Mustard, and D. J. Sridhar, "The Enrollment Effects of Merit-Based Financial Aid: Evidence from Georgia's HOPE Program," *Journal of Labor Economics* 24:761–86 (2006).

40. Lora Cohen-Vogel et al., "The Spread of Merit Based College Aid," *Education Policy* 22:3 (2008): 339–62.

41. In 2003, Riley proposed a 22 percent increase in state taxes to fund improvements in schools. It was soundly defeated, mainly because agribusinesses opposed to increased taxation ran commercials arguing it would be bad for African Americans. See David Halbfinger, "G.O.P. Chief's Idea for Raising Alabama: Taxes," *New York Times,* June 4, 2003, http://www.nytimes.com/2003/06/04/us/gop-chief-s-idea-for-raising-alabama-taxes.html, accessed September 3, 2010.

THREE. THE GEOGRAPHY OF POVERTY

1. Carol Stack documents this return migration in her volume *Call to Home*. She notes that what we once took to be a one-way migration from south to north was actually a protracted circle that brought African Americans back to the region they thought of as home when their elderly relatives were in need of help. She argued this was not inspired by economic opportunity so much as by kin obligation. The poor families we interviewed did have kin in the area, but they moved to the South because the jobs were moving out from under them in the North. See Carol Stack, *Call to Home: African Americans Reclaim the Rural South* (New York: Basic Books, 1996).

2. Jing Fang, Shantha Madhavan, and Michael H. Alderman, "The Association between Birthplace and Mortality from Cardiovascular Causes among Black and White Residents of New York City," *New England Journal of Medicine* 335 (1996): 1545–51.

3. We generally define "the South" as including Virginia, West Virginia, North Carolina, South Carolina, Georgia, Florida, Alabama, Mississippi, Tennessee, Kentucky, Arkansas, Louisiana, Oklahoma, and Texas.

4. Alemayehu Bishaw and Jessica Smega, *Income, Earnings, and Poverty Data from the 2007 American Community Survey* (Washington, DC: U.S. Census Bureau, 2008), http://www.census.gov/prod/2008pubs/acs-09.pdf, accessed on May 24, 2010.

5. Greg J. Duncan, W. Jean Yeung, Jeanne Brooks-Gunn, and Judith R. Smith, "How Much Does Childhood Poverty Affect the Life Chances of Children?" *American Sociological Review* 63(3): (June 1998): 406–23.

6. For a more detailed discussion of the impact of childhood poverty on life chances, including health and educational achievement, see Greg Duncan and Jeanne Brooks-Gunn, *Consequences of Growing Up Poor* (New York: Russell Sage Foundation, 1997).

7. One particularly serious form of material hardship is food insecurity: running out of food before the end of the month. Data from the Current Population Survey charts the prevalence of families that experience this hardship. While we have not controlled for household income here, it is a safe assumption that food insecurity is a far more

serious problem for the poor than anyone else, hence we are probably looking at the prevalence of scarcity among low-income households. In every southern state except for Florida, Virginia, and West Virginia, more than 12 percent of poor households experienced food insecurity between 2003 and 2005. In Mississippi, Texas, and South Carolina, the rates were 16.5 percent, 16 percent, and 15.5 percent, respectively, well above the national average of 11.4 percent. It seems likely, then, that the lower cost of living does not protect the southern poor from this risk. See Mark Nord, Margaret Andrews, and Steven Carolson, *Houehold Food Security in the United States, 2005*, Economic Research Report No. ERR-29 (Washington, DC: U.S. Department of Agriculture, 2006), http://www.ers.usda.gov/Publications/ERR29/ERR29i.pdf, accessed on May 24, 2010.

8. India Together, Infant Mortality across India (Bangalore), http://www.indiatogether.org/photo/2003/inf-mortal.htm, accessed July 10, 2009.

9. Information on the infant and adult complications of low birth weight is provided in the March of Dimes fact sheets for professionals and researchers, available at http://www.marchofdimes.com/professionals/14332_1153.asp#head5, accessed July 12, 2009.

10. See Kristin Luker, *Dubious Conceptions: The Politics of Teenage Pregnancy* (Cambridge: Harvard University Press, 1997).

11. Teenage pregnancy and out-of-wedlock childbearing should not be conflated, as Kristin Luker's work in *Dubious Conceptions* makes clear. A lot of teen moms are married, and this may be more prevalent in the South than elsewhere. Still, being a teen mom is likely to have an impact on the educational attainment of mothers and their young spouses. See S. McLanahan and G. D. Sandefur, *Growing Up with a Single Parent: What Hurts, What Helps* (Cambridge: Harvard University Press, 1994) for an extensive discussion of this issue.

12. The health status of children in the South has attracted the attention of epidemiologists who are now focusing more attention on the role of regional disparities. For more on this topic, see Jeffrey Goldhagen et al., "The Health Status of Southern Children: A Neglected Regional Disparity," *Pediatrics* 116:6 (2005): 746–53, available online at

http://pediatrics.aappublications.org/cgi/content/abstract/116/6/e746, accessed May 24, 2010.

13. Heart disease is perhaps less regionally concentrated, but it still exhibits a worrying level within the southern region. New York and Missouri join the roster of states like Mississippi, Alabama, Arkansas, Oklahoma, and Kentucky in exhibiting high rates of death due to heart disease. See statehealthfacts.org (Menlo Park, CA: Kaiser Family Foundation), http://www.statehealthfacts.org/comparemaptable.jsp?ind=77&cat=2, accessed July 12, 2009.

14. See statehealthfacts.org (Menlo Park, CA: Kaiser Family Foundation), http://www.statehealthfacts.org/comparemaptable.jsp?ind=92&cat=2, accessed July 12, 2009.

15. See Katherine S. Newman, *A Different Shade of Gray: Midlife and Beyond in the Inner City* (New York: New Press, 2003) for a discussion of the emergence of chronic disease associated with the elder years among the middle-aged residents of inner city New York. She notes that stress and poor medical care contribute to premature aging, which entails the emergence of life-threatening illness much earlier than is typical of more-affluent populations.

16. The research done by the MacArthur Foundation's Network on Social Economic Status and Health has made this point many times over in its ground-breaking work on inequality and health disparities. For an overview, consult MacArthur Foundation (Chicago, IL), http://www.macfound.org/site/c.lkLXJ8MQKrH/b.951947/k.11B4/Research_Networks__Socioeconomic_Status_and_Health.htm, accessed July 12, 2009.

17. For data comparing health outcomes across states for blacks, see appendix II.

18. See appendix II for data on health outcomes by race for each state.

19. Goldhagen et al. have investigated this question in their quest to understand the role of region of residence in children's health outcomes. They conclude that independent of the variables such as idleness (not attending school or working), the absence of a full-time working parent in the house, and percent of the state that is African

American, a robust relationship between southern residence and a low score on their "child health index" remains. See Goldhagen et al., "The Health Status of Southern Children: A Neglected Regional Disparity," *Pediatrics* 116:6 (December 2005): 746–53, online at http://pediatrics.aappublications.org/cgi/content/abstract/116/6/e746, accessed July 12, 2009.

20. See, for example, I. Kawachi, B. P. Kennedy, and R. G. Wilkinson, *Income Inequality and Health* (New York: New Press, 1999).

21. A. Deaton and D. Lubotsky, "Mortality, Inequality and Race in American Cities and States," *Social Science & Medicine* 56 (2003): 1139–53.

22. See M. Ash and D. E. Robinson, "Inequality, Race, and Mortality in U.S. Cities: A Political and Econometric Review," *Social Science & Medicine* 68:11 (June 2009): 1914–17.

23. Richard Murnane and Frank Levy, *Teaching the New Basic Skills: Principles for Educating Children to Thrive in a Changing Economy* (New York: Free Press, 1996).

24. For a thorough account of this change as it unfolded throughout the twentieth century, see especially Claudia Goldin and Lawrence Katz, *The Race between Education and Technology* (Cambridge: Harvard University Press, 2008).

25. If we flip the question and ask about the percentage of the adult population with a bachelor's degree, we see similarly problematic regional disparities: 38 percent of the adults in Massachusetts have a BA; in the Deep South, the rates run the gamut, but it's a shorter gamut. Only 17 percent of West Virginia's citizens have college diplomas, while 21 percent do in Tennessee. Even North Carolina, home to the powerhouse Research Triangle Park, boasts an overall rate of only 26 percent with college degrees. These gaps matter because they tell potential employers where they can recruit a high-tech or white collar workforce easily and where they can't.

26. Bruce Western, *Punishment and Inequality in America* (New York: Russell Sage Foundation, 2007), p. 27.

27. Bureau of Justice Statistics. U.S. Department of Justice. Crime Trends, http://bjs.ojp.usdoj.gov/dataonline/Search/Crime/Crime.cfm, accessed September 3, 2010.

28. U.S. Census Bureau, The 2010 Statistical Abstract (Law Enforcement, Courts and Prisons: Crime and Crime Rates), www.census.gov/ compendia/statab/cats/law_enforcement_courts_prisons/crimes_and _crime_rates.html, accessed May 24, 2010.

29. Besiki Kutateladze, *Is America Really So Punitive? Exploring a Continuum of U.S. State Criminal Justice Policies* (El Paso, TX: Lfb Scholarly Publishing, 2009).

30. Richard Freeman, "The Economics of Crime," in *Handbook of Labor Economics,* ed. Orley Ashenfelter and David Cards, vol. 3, chap. 52 (Amsterdam: North Holland Publishers, 1999) and Richard B. Freeman, "Why Do So Many Young American Men Commit Crimes and What Might We Do about It?" *Journal of Economic Perspectives* 10:1 (1996): 25–42.

31. See Kutateladze.

FOUR. TAX TRAPS AND REGIONAL POVERTY REGIMES

1. The data used for estimation were updated to 2008 in collaboration with Kevin Hassett and colleagues at the American Enterprise Institute. We summarize the estimation procedure below; for additional details, see Kevin Hassett and Anne Moore, *How Do Tax Policies Affect Low Income Workers?* American Enterprise Institute for Public Policy Research Working Paper no. 121, December 2005, http://www.aei.org/docLib/20051208_WP121.pdf.

2. See National Bureau of Economic Research, TAXSIM Related Files at the NBER (Cambridge, MA), http://www.nber.org/~taxsim, accessed May 24, 2010, and Daniel Feenberg and Elisabeth Coutts, "An Introduction to the TAXSIM Model," *Journal of Policy Analysis and Management* 12:1 (Winter 1993).

3. To ensure that the National Bureau of Economic Research's TAXSIM was truly capturing state income tax liability net of offsetting credits and deductions, we double-checked their estimates by running the details of a hypothetical family through commercial tax preparation software for each of the fifty states for the 2008 tax year.

We found the estimated tax liability generated by the commercial tax software matched closely with the results from the bureau's model.

4. Alaska has been excluded from this analysis because of its complicated local sales tax structure and the variation in payments to residents from the Alaska Permanent Fund (oil profits).

5. To be sure, the expenditures of a household at the poverty line will vary both across and within states. Localized spending patterns, however, are also extremely likely to be influenced in part by the prevailing tax rates. Using a national aggregate measure allows us to avoid this problem of endogeneity to get a more accurate sense of the relative regressivity of each state's tax system.

6. Localities exact their own sales taxes, in addition to those demanded by the states. As rates can vary from one place to the next within a state, Hassett and Moore estimated a weighted average by looking at total state and local sales tax receipts within a state and determining what the averaged local rate must be to generate the gap in revenue not accounted for by the state rate.

7. Typical "cross-section" regression analysis—the workhorse of the social sciences—uses data from a single point in time to determine whether there is some association between the outcome of interest (y) and the primary predictor (x) over and above any competing explanations that we can eliminate by controlling for them in our model. Cross-sectional associations are seldom deemed causal because it is impossible to disentangle what causes what. Consider the case of mortality and taxes on the poor. A simple cross-sectional model regressing mortality on tax burden may find a statistically significant relationship net of a host of controls such as state poverty rate, racial composition, and so on. But there could be another factor we have not considered that could be driving the relationship: perhaps, for example, citizens in states that tax the poor also indulge in fatty fried foods. If this is the case, our cross-sectional models would point to a relationship between taxes and mortality that doesn't actually exist and wouldn't show up if we could control for the right (but unobservable or unmeasured) characteristics of the state. One way to deal with problems of "unobserved heterogeneity"—that is, potentially relevant explanatory factors that are not observed and there-

fore cannot be controlled for directly—is to use fixed-effects models that require longitudinal data.

8. For a review of the recent literature on crime, income, and labor markets, see David B. Mustard, "How Do Labor Markets Affect Crime? New Evidence on an Old Puzzle," in *Handbook on the Economics of Crime*, ed. B. L. Benson and P. R. Zimmerman (Northampton, MA: Edward Elgar Publishing, 2010).

9. It may be argued that we are "over controlling" in these models, that is, that by including measures such as the state poverty rate, we are actually stealing away the variation that could otherwise be explained by our tax predictor. However, as our primary aim is to demonstrate a plausible association between taxing the poor and the poverty-related outcomes we test, we decided to control for any reasonable alternative explanations. The state's poverty rate, for example, provides information on the distribution of household income in the state that is distinct from what we can glean from mean income or state GDP, and therefore we thought it important to include.

10. In alternative model specifications, we used a more narrow measure of state spending that aggregated all "social spending," including health, education, and welfare. The choice of control had no substantive impact on our results.

11. The approximately twenty-five-year period covered by our data also coincided with a dramatic decrease in the percentage of smoking adults and a shift in the demography of smokers. It could be argued that the changing demography of smoking over this period could account for differential changes in age-adjusted mortality. To account for this, we estimated additional models that included a variable on the percent of adults who smoke by state, taken from the CDC. Unfortunately, state-level smoking data were not available for as far back as 1982, so they do not cover the entire period analyzed in our models. We were therefore only able to test whether the inclusion of percent of adults who smoke by state in 1990 and 2005 affected that limited two-point fixed-effects model. The inclusion of this control for smoking had no substantive effect on our models.

12. First, we performed a number of tests to ensure that our "tax

effect" was not being driven by a handful of states with extreme values. To guard against a purely "southern effect," we ran the fixed-effects models on the subset of non-southern states and attained results substantively similar to the full model. To further test for any potential outliers, we also performed the analysis on three random draws of thirty-six states and again attained substantively similar results. Second, we used alternative specifications for time trends, including year as a continuous term (instead of a set of dummy variables), year as a quadratic term, and region-specific time trends, each with substantively similar results. Indeed, many of these alternative model specifications actually improved the statistical significance of the tax coefficient (lowered the p-value), but we chose to report results from the more conservative full state and year fixed-effects models.

13. Measuring high school completion is fraught with complications. Different and evolving standards of what constitutes graduation (diplomas versus GED certificates, for example) and differential reporting patterns at the state and local level make it difficult to compare graduation statistics across states, let alone across time, which is pivotal to our fixed-effects analysis. To get around these measurement errors, we took our data on high school completion from John R. Warren, an education researcher at the University of Minnesota, who has constructed a measure of high school completion that is explicitly designed to be comparable across states and across years, making it ideal for our fixed-effects analysis. See John Robert Warren, "State-Level High School Completion Rates: Concepts, Measures, and Trends," *Education Policy Analysis Archives,* http://epaa.asu.edu/ojs/article/viewFile/156/282, accessed May 24, 2010.

14. John Robert Warren, "State-Level High School Completion Rates: Concepts, Measures, and Trends," *Education Policy Analysis Archives,* http://epaa.asu.edu/ojs/article/viewFile/156/282, accessed May 24, 2010.

15. Sara Mclanahan and Christine Percheski, "Family Structure and the Reproduction of Inequality," *Annual Review of Sociology* 34 (2008): 257–76.

16. Susan Mayer, *What Money Can't Buy: Family Income and Children's Life Chances* (Cambridge: Harvard University Press, 1998).

17. Christopher Jencks and Susan Mayer, "The Social Consequences of Growing Up in a Poor Neighborhood," in *Inner-City Poverty in the United States,* ed. Laurence Lynn and Michael McGeary, p. 111–86 (Washington, DC: National Academies Press, 1990).

18. Jencks and Mayer (ibid.) provide an exhaustive review of the literature on neighborhood effects, examining especially how educational attainment, cognitive skills, criminal activity, sexual behavior, and labor market success is affected by the socioeconomic status composition of neighborhoods and schools. They point out that the evidence is very mixed and ofttimes there but weak, plagued with measurement problems.

19. David Harding, *Living the Drama: Community, Conflict and Culture among Inner City Boys* (Chicago: University of Chicago Press, 2010).

20. These effects are not due to differences between states in the general economic climate, or in unemployment, nor were they reflections of fluctuations in state spending. In our models, yearly unemployment and the state-level GDP per capita were controlled statistically, as were state expenditures. The impact of taxing the poor that we observed occurred over and above the effects of economic downturns, unemployment, and government spending.

21. Connecticut's Jobs First; the Newswick and British Columbia sites of the Canadian Self-Sufficiency Project; the Los Angeles Jobs First GAIN; and the Atlanta, GA, Grand Rapids, MI, and Riverside, CA, sites for the National Evaluation of Welfare to Work Strategies provide data on more than 8,000 children age two to five when the experiments began. G. Duncan, P. Morris, and C. Rodrigues, Does Money Really Matter? Estimating Impacts of Family Income on Children's Achievement with Data from Social Policy Experiments (manuscript, 2008) (New York: MDRC), p. 7–8.

22. Measured through reports from parents or teachers or more objective measures like test scores.

23. Morris et al., p. 16.

24. Randall Akee et al., "Parents' Incomes and Children's Outcomes: A Quasi-Experiment Using Transfer Payments from Casino Profits," *American Economic Journal: Applied Economics* 2:1 (2010): 85–115.

25. The children were ages nine, eleven, and thirteen; they were followed annually until they turned sixteen and then reinterviewed at nineteen and twenty-one.

26. Akee et al.

27. Gordon Dahl and Lance Lochner, *The Impact of Family Income on Child Achievement: Evidence from the Earned Income Tax Credit,* Working Paper 145999 (Cambridge, MA: National Bureau of Economic Research, 2008).

28. Ibid., p. 2.

29. Ibid., p. 18.

30. Kathryn Edin et al. Investing in Enduring Resources with the Earned Income Tax Credit. Unpublished manuscript, Harvard University (2010).

31. See, for example, Adam Drewnowski and S. E. Specter, "Poverty and Obesity: The Role of Energy Density and Energy Costs," *American Journal of Clinical Nutrition* 79:1 (January 2004): 6–16.

32. For a primer on TANF financing and eligibility, see *Policy Basics: An Introduction to TANF* (Washington, DC: Center on Budget and Policy Priorities, 2009), http://www.cbpp.org/cms/index.cfm?fa=view&id=936, accessed August 11, 2009.

33. Liz Schott and Zachary Levinson, *TANF Benefits Are Low and Have Not Kept Pace with Inflation* (Washington, DC: Center on Budget and Policy Priorities, 2008), http://www.cbpp.org/pdf/11-24-08tanf.pdf, accessed August 11, 2009.

34. Between 1996 and 2008, the real dollar value of TANF benefits declined in forty-seven states. Some southern states, including Florida, Georgia, North Carolina, and Tennessee, saw their benefit levels drop by more than 26 percent while others, such as South Carolina and Alabama, saw declines of only 3.2 percent and 3.5 percent, respectively. Mississippi actually saw a 4.2 percent increase in the real value of TANF benefits during this period (ibid). It is important to note, however, that the benefit levels in these states are already considerably lower than in other parts of the country.

35. Missouri Economic Research and Information Center (MERIC), *State Cost of Living Indices for the 1st quarter of 2009,* http://www.missouri

economy.org/indicators/cost_of_living/index.stm, accessed August 10, 2009. For original data on city cost of living indices, see Council for Community and Economic Research, *ACCRA Cost of Living Index* (Arlington, VA), http://www.coli.org/default.asp, accessed August 10, 2009.

36. In 2004–2005, state government provided 46.9 percent of education revenues. Local governments provided 44.0 percent, and the federal government provided 9.2 percent. See U.S. Department of Education, *Digest of Education Statistics,* Table 162, http://nces.ed.gov/Programs/digest, accessed September 3, 2010. For a discussion of kindergarten-through-twelfth-grade education financing, see K. Carey and M. Roza, *School Funding's Tragic Flaw* (Seattle: University of Washington, Center on Reinventing Public Education and Education Sector, 2008).

37. New America Foundation, Federal Education Budget Project, Per Pupil Expenditure (2007), http://febp.newamerica.net/k12/rankings/ppexpend07, accessed on May 24, 2010.

38. For a detailed discussion of trends in the departure of affluent whites to private schools in southern states since the late 1960s, see Stephen H. Wainscott, "Consequences of Southern School Desegregation: Myth and Reality," in *The Disappearing South: Studies in Regional Change and Continuity,* ed. Robert P. Steed, Laurence W. Moreland, and Tod A. Baker (Tuscaloosa: University of Alabama Press, 1990).

39. Susan Mayer and Leonard Lopoo, "Government Spending and Intergenerational Mobility," *Journal of Public Economics* 92 (2008): 139–58.

40. Ibid., p. 144.

FIVE. THE BOTTOM LINE

1. See Katherine Newman and Elisabeth Jacobs, *Who Cares? Public Ambivalence and Government Activism from the New Deal to the Second Gilded Age* (Princeton: Princeton University Press, 2010), and also see B. Steensland, *The Failed Welfare Revolution: America's Struggle over Guaranteed Income Policy* (Princeton: Princeton University Press, 2008).

2. While much federal spending in the South is in the form of military bases and other defense appropriations, the states of the old Confederacy generally receive as much as the Northeast in terms of retirement,

disability, health, and welfare spending despite paying much less in the way of federal taxes. See *Flow of Federal Funds to States* (Washington, DC: Northeast-Midwest Institute), http://www.nemw.org/index.php/flow-of-federal-funds, and their "Table 2. Per-Capita Federal Spending: Fiscal 2008," http://www.nemw.org/images/fedspend2.pdf, accessed May 24, 2010.

3. Pedro Carneiro and James Heckman, "Human Capital Policy," in *Inequality in America: What Role for Human Capital Policies?* ed. J. Heckman and A. Kruger (Cambridge, MA: MIT Press, 2003).

4. Our data for mortality, for example, cover years 1982 to 2005, so we averaged tax burdens over that period; property crime and violent crime covered years 1982 to 2006, and teenage pregnancy covered years 1988 to 2000.

5. We completed a similar analysis on our other outcome variables from the fixed-effects models. All of them came out statistically significant, but the coefficients were tiny, and hence we make no claims for them other than to note that the direction of the effect is the same as for the other outcomes of interest. The results of these analyses can be found in appendix II.

6. Between 1982 and 2005, the average tax burden for a family of three in the South was $382.24 compared with $45.44 in the northeast states, a difference of $336.80. If we multiply that number by the tax coefficient in our fixed-effects model for mortality from chapter 4, we get $336.8 \times 0.067 = -22.57$. This means that had the South taxed the poor at the same rate as the Northeast—and changed nothing else—state-level, age-adjusted mortality would have declined an additional 22.46 per 100,000 in the southern states. See appendix II for the actual estimates.

CONCLUSION

1. For a detailed treatment of this issue see Katherine Newman and Elisabeth Jacobs, *Who Cares? Public Ambivalence and Government Activism from the New Deal to the Second Gilded Age* (Princeton: Princeton University Press, 2010).

2. Andrea Campbell, *What the Social Security Experience Tells Us about Taxes Americans Can Embrace* (Washington, DC: Scholar's Strategy Network, January 2010), http://www.scholarsstrategynetwork.org/pdfs/Taxes_Americans_Can%20Embrace-Andrea_Campbell.pdf.

3. T. Skocpol, "Targeting within Universalism: Politically Viable Policies to Combat Poverty in the United States," in *The Urban Underclass,* ed. C. Jencks and P. E. Peterson (Washington, DC: Brookings Institution, 1991), p. 411–36.

4. Income taxes require lump-sum payments by the self-employed and the very wealthy, but for most Americans the process of collecting the income tax is exactly like social security: it is withheld from every paycheck.

5. Lawrence Jacobs, *Escaping the Fiscal Death Spiral and Overcoming Anti-Tax Conservatism* (Washington, DC: Scholar's Strategy Network, January 2010), http://www.scholarsstrategynetwork.org/pdfs/Escaping _the_Fiscal_Death_Spiral-Lawrence_Jacobs.pdf. See also Catherine Rampell, "Many See the VAT Option as a Cure for Deficits," *New York Times,* December 10, 2009, http://www.nytimes.com/2009/12/11/business/11vat.html, accessed September 3, 2010.

6. Nicholas Johnson and Erica Williams, *Some States Scaling Back Tax Credits for Low-Income Families* (Washington, DC: Center on Budget and Policy Priorities, 2010), http://www.cbpp.org/files/4-29-10sfp.pdf, accessed May 24, 2010.

7. Pedro Carneiro and James Heckman, "Human Capital Policy," in *Inequality in America: What Role for Human Capital Policies?* ed. J. Heckman and A. Kruger (Cambridge, MA: MIT Press, 2003).

8. Y. Yilmaz, S. Hoo, M. Nagowski, K. Rueben, and R. Tannenwald, *Measuring Fiscal Disparities across the US States: A Representative Revenue System/Representative Expenditure System Approach, Fiscal Year 2002,* Working Paper 06–2 (Boston: Federal Reserve Bank of Boston, New England Public Policy Center, 2006).

9. Just as the Centers for Medicaid and Medicare Services at the Department of Health and Human Services in Washington adjusts Medicare reimbursement rates using regional cost-of-living scales.

INDEX

Page numbers followed by *f* indicate figures, page numbers followed by *t* indicate tables, and page numbers followed by *m* indicate maps.

Text:	10.75/15 Janson
Display:	Janson
Compositor:	BookMatters, Berkeley
Indexer:	Leonard Rosenbaum
Printer and binder:	Sheridan Books, Inc.

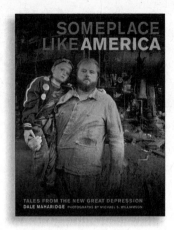

Falling from Grace

Downward Mobility in the Age of Affluence

KATHERINE S. NEWMAN

"Searches beyond the statistics of economic decline, plant closings, layoffs, and unemployment to capture the drama of human suffering at the individual level."

—**Bart Landry,** *Contemporary Sociology*

Honorable Mention, C. Wright Mills Award
$24.95 paper 978-0-520-21842-0

Poverty in America

A Handbook

JOHN ICELAND

Second Edition with a New Preface

"With succinct and engaging prose, *Poverty in America* covers the gamut—from theoretical issues to measurement to history to public policy—better than any other book out there right now."

—**Dalton Conley, author of *Honky***

$24.95 paper 978-0-520-24841-0

www.ucpress.edu

Someplace Like America

Tales from the New Great Depression

DALE MAHARIDGE

Photographs by Michael Williamson

This brilliant and essential study—begun in the trickle-down Reagan years and culminating with the recent banking catastrophe—puts a human face on today's grim economic numbers through shoe leather reporting, memoir, vivid stories, stunning photographs, and thoughtful analysis.
$27.50 cloth 978-0-520-26247-8

Uninsured in America

Life and Death in the Land of Opportunity

SUSAN STARR SERED and RUSHIKA FERNANDOPULLE

Updated with a New Afterword

"A vivid, indignant, and important book, and it does one thing better than any other before…makes the abandoned millions visible again." —**Atul Gawande, MD, author of *Complications***

$17.95 paper 978-0-520-25006-2